At Issue

| Athlete Activism

Other Books in the At Issue Series

At Issue

Athlete Activism

Gary Wiener, Book Editor

GREENHAVEN
PUBLISHING

Published in 2020 by Greenhaven Publishing, LLC
353 3rd Avenue, Suite 255, New York, NY 10010

Articles in Greenhaven Publishing anthologies are often edited for length to meet page
requirements. In addition, original titles of these works are changed to clearly present
the main thesis and to explicitly indicate the author's opinion. Every effort is made to
ensure that Greenhaven Publishing accurately reflects the original intent of the authors.
Every effort has been made to trace the owners of the copyrighted material.

Cover image: OSTILL is Franck Camhi/Shutterstock.com (silhouetted
football player), Lisa Kolbasa/Shutterstock.com (background figures)

Library of Congress Cataloging-in-Publication Data

Names: Wiener, Gary, editor.
Title: Athlete activism / Gary Wiener, book editor.
Description: First edition. | New York : Greenhaven Publishing, 2020. | Series: At
issue | Includes bibliographical references and index. | Audience: Grades 9–12.
Identifiers: LCCN 2019022815 | ISBN 9781534506350 (library
binding) | ISBN 9781534506343 (paperback)
Subjects: LCSH: Sports—Political aspects—United States—Juvenile literature. |
Professional athletes—United States—Political activity—Juvenile literature. | Racism in
sports—United States—Juvenile literature. | Discrimination in sports—United States—
Juvenile literature. | Social media in sports—United States—Juvenile literature.
Classification: LCC GV706.35 .A84 2020 | DDC 306.4/83—dc23
LC record available at https://lccn.loc.gov/2019022815

Manufactured in the United States of America

Website: http://greenhavenpublishing.com

Contents

Introduction

There are certain key moments in history when athletics and social issues coalesced in such a way that these events have become part of American popular culture. Track and field star Jesse Owens' victory in the 1936 Olympics refuted Adolf Hitler's insistence on Aryan superiority; Tommie Smith's and John Carlos' raised fists on the 1968 Olympic medalists' podium protested the treatment of African-Americans in the United States; boxing champion Muhammad Ali's refusal to fight in the Vietnam War was a similar protest that made him a polarizing figure in our country.

More recently there was the arresting sight of Colin Kaepernick kneeling during the national anthem before a 2016 NFL pre-season game. No athletic gesture in recent memory has kicked off such an avalanche of conflicting opinions. In the wake of a number of police shootings of unarmed African American men and boys, Kaepernick decided to make a stand: "I am not looking for approval," he said. "I have to stand up for people that are oppressed."[1]

Kaepernick's actions divided the nation. Many have argued that Kaepernick's gesture is offensive to the United States in general and the military in particular. Others would suggest that such ideas are a misinterpretation of Kaepernick's gesture. Ironically, Kaepernick had no intention of offending those who protect the United States. After his original gesture of sitting during the anthem as a protest, Kaepernick was contacted by former Seattle Seahawks player and US Army Green Beret Nate Boyer. The two spoke, and it was Boyer who suggested that Kaepernick kneel during the anthem. "We sorta came to a middle ground where he would take a knee alongside his teammates," Boyer said. "Soldiers take a knee in front of a fallen brother's grave, you know, to show respect."[2] And so, Kaepenick did. Still, the criticism ramped up.

Even the president of the United States weighed in. At a political rally in Alabama, Donald Trump made these profane, and many believe, un-presidential, remarks: "Wouldn't you love to see one of these NFL owners, when somebody disrespects our flag, to say, 'Get that son of a bitch off the field right now?'" Trump asked his audience. "Out. He's fired. He's fired."[3]

Political protest, especially by athletes, and even more so by minority athletes, has always met with resistance, and it is undeniable that athletes who take a stand, whether one approves of their methods and causes or not, display a certain amount of bravery.

After all, Jesse Owens thumbed his nose at Hitler in Nazi Germany. Tommie Smith and John Carlos were ostracized for their protest and they and their families received death threats; Muhammad Ali was banned from boxing for refusing to fight in Vietnam; and Colin Kaepernick has been seemingly blacklisted by NFL owners. Despite having starred in Super Bowl XLVII, Kaepernick can find no takers among the NFL's thirty-two teams.

Nevertheless, Kaepernick's protest has had a profound effect on American society and politics. Love him or hate him, he has not only opened up, or re-opened, the American conversation on race, but he has also inspired a new generation of young athletes who are not afraid to speak up when necessary. Prominent sports website The Athletic went so far as to label 2017 "The Year of Athletes and Activism," noting that even while Kaepernick sat out of football and remained relatively quiet, he had been turned into something of a martyr; that LeBron James had worn basketball shoes that spelled out "equality"; that Steph Curry and the NBA champion Golden State Warriors had declined an invitation to appear at the White House; that members of the WNBA's Los Angeles Sparks stayed in the locker room when the National Anthem was played during the league finals; and that J. T. Brown of the NHL's The Tampa Bay Lightning "became the first NHL player to raise his fist during the anthem before a game against the Florida Panthers on Oct. 7."[4]

None of these gestures was, according to these athletes, designed to be disrespectful to the flag or the military. They were meant to protest unjust conditions and racial profiling in the United States, where unarmed black men were often being shot by police. As Los Angeles Sparks star player Candace Parker explained:

> *This is not a protest against America or against the flag. I feel I can't kneel before the flag; I have too much respect and pride to do that. There are some people who can. There are some people on our team we don't want to have to make that choice. We didn't want to put anyone in an awkward position. In this, we're united. We're still respecting the United States and the flag, but still taking a stand.*[5]

Even so, such protests have sparked controversy and elicited hatred from those who deliberately choose to ignore the message and focus on the method. This sort of activism will inevitably face pushback of the kind seen in Minneapolis. When Cleveland Browns wide receiver Andrew Hawkins wore a shirt that said, "Justice for Tamir Rice And John Crawford III" before a game in December 2014 to protest the deaths of two unarmed African Americans, Jeff Follmer, president of the Cleveland Police Patrolman's Association, said:

> *It's pretty pathetic when athletes think they know the law. They should stick to what they know best on the field. The Cleveland Police protect and serve the Browns stadium and the Browns organization owes us an apology.*[6]

Follmer was not alone in his views. He was re-elected union chief three years later.

In 2016, members of the WNBA's Minnesota Lynx wore black shirts that read, "Change starts with us, justice and accountability." On the back of the shirts were the names Philando Castile and Alton Sterling, victims of police shootings, and the words "Black Lives Matter." The shirts also bore the crest of the Dallas Police Department, which lost five of its officers to senseless retaliatory violence. But four off-duty members of the Minneapolis Police Department, who were providing private security, quit due to the athlete's activism. The president of the union that represents

Minneapolis police officers, praised them for walking off the job, saying that "If [the players] are going to keep their stance, all officers may refuse to work there."[7]

The conservative media, along with some fans, have also fueled a backlash against athlete activism. One Buffalo Bills fan held a sign that read, "Don't you dare KNEEL for my anthem. Go Bills."[8] When NFL viewership was down in 2016 and 2017, many were quick to blame the anthem controversy. But many other factors could also have contributed: poor matchups, the rise of streaming services, poor play by teams in major markets, etc. And viewership rebounded in 2018, even as some players continued to protest.

As opposed to the past, when sports personalities were often cowed by protest and the fear of losing popularity or their jobs, fewer athletes are backing down from their activism. They have answered their critics by refusing to just shut up and play.

Athlete activism is not just about protest. One major positive that has come out of recent athlete activism is that many sports figures have stepped up their game in providing influential community outreach. LeBron James started a school for underprivileged youth in his hometown of Akron, Ohio; Colin Kaepernick runs a foundation dedicated to raising awareness about higher education, self-empowerment, and proper interaction with law enforcement; and countless other athletes are forces for good in their communities.

At Issue: Athlete Activism seeks to investigate the ways in which both yesterday's and today's athletes have sought and continue to seek ways to be role models, to change society for the better, and to stand up to negativity to do so. The viewpoints included provide a wide range of perspectives that investigate what it means when a sportswoman or man attempts to be more than just an athlete.

Endnotes

1. Kofie Yeboah, "A Timeline of Events Since Colin Kaepernick's National Anthem Protest," The Undefeated, September 6, 2016. http://theundefeated.com/features/a-timeline-of-events-since-colin-kaepernicks-national-anthem-protest/

2. Will Brinson, "Here's How Nate Boyer Got Colin Kaepernick to Go From Sitting to Kneeling," CBS Sports. September 27, 2016. https://www.cbssports.com/nfl/news/heres-how-nate-boyer-got-colin-kaepernick-to-go-from-sitting-to-kneeling/

3. "Trump on Kaepernick: 'Get That Son of a Bitch Off the Field,'" The Week, September 23, 2017. https://theweek.com/speedreads/726627/trump-kaepernick-that-son-bitch-field

4. Jerry Bembry, "The Year of Athletes and Activism," The Undefeated. December 29, 2017. https://theundefeated.com/features/2017-the-year-of-athletes-and-activism/

5. Jerry Bembry, "The Year of Athletes and Activism," The Undefeated. December 29, 2017. https://theundefeated.com/features/2017-the-year-of-athletes-and-activism/

6. Matt Vasilogambros, "When Athletes Take Political Stands," *The Atlantic*, July 12, 2016. https://www.theatlantic.com/news/archive/2016/07/when-athletes-take-political-stands/490967/

7. Matt Vasilogambros, "When Athletes Take Political Stands," *The Atlantic*, July 12, 2016. https://www.theatlantic.com/news/archive/2016/07/when-athletes-take-political-stands/490967/

8. Brett Carlsen, "Arizona Cardinals v Buffalo Bills," Getty Images, September 25, 2016. https://www.gettyimages.com/detail/news-photo/fan-holds-a-sign-referencing-various-professional-players-news-photo/610385502

1

Athlete Activism Is On the Rise, But So Is the Backlash

Larry Platt

Larry Platt is the co-founder and editor of The Philadelphia Citizen, *a nonprofit news site, and is co-author of the* New York Times *memoir* Every Day I Fight. *His work has appeared in* GQ, *the* New York Times Magazine, New York, Men's Journal, *and Salon.com, among other publications.*

Athletes have long spoken out on political matters, but in the past were often shunned for their activism. Speaking out hurt Muhammad Ali's popularity during his career, and Charles Barkley claims he lost millions due to his penchant for telling it like it is. But lately there has been a change. Barkley and Ali are now beloved figures and LeBron James, arguably the greatest athlete alive, has been vocal on societal issues and free spending in his charitable pursuits. According to Platt, "Establishment forces ... have come to endorse, or at least grin and bear, athlete activism." Still, backlash is increasing. President Donald Trump and conservative media figures have attempted to squelch outspoken athletes. But today's athletes are more media savvy and able to hold their own in the face of criticism. They may not yet be able to change the system, but they can raise awareness and create a dialogue around social inequities.

"Athlete Activism Is on the Rise, But So Is the Backlash," by Larry Platt, GlobalSport Matters, April 16, 2018. Reprinted by permission. GlobalSport Matters is a joint initiative between Arizona State University's Global Sport Institute and the Walter Cronkite School of Journalism and Mass Communication.

I n March, the Charles Barkley who hosted *Saturday Night Live* was a faint image of the Charles Barkley who spoke out on political issues in the early '90s. The current Barkley is a cuddly class clown who is, not coincidentally, much more beloved than when, as an NBA all-star 25 years ago, he'd hold court on political matters in the locker room of the Philadelphia 76ers.

"Just because you give Charles Barkley a lot of money, it doesn't mean I'm not going to voice my opinions," he lectured the media throng around him back then. "Me getting 20 rebounds ain't important. We've got people homeless on our streets and the media is crowding around my locker. It's ludicrous."

At the time, his friend and rival, Michael Jordan, explained his unwillingness to endorse a credible black challenger to right-wing Senator Jesse Helms in his home state of North Carolina by saying "Republicans buy sneakers, too." Barkley's response was to pose on the cover of the hip-hop basketball magazine *SLAM* with Spike Lee, proclaiming themselves to be "Nineties N****s." "I don't have to be what you want me to be," Barkley said to the sportswriters chronicling him, echoing a Muhammad Ali line from the '60s.

Now here he was on the set of *SNL*, just a few months after stumping for Democrat Doug Jones' Senate election in his native state of Alabama ("at some point, we gotta stop looking like idiots to the nation"), and just days after Fox News' Laura Ingraham had told LeBron James to "shut up and dribble" after he'd deigned to talk about social justice. "A lot of athletes are worried that speaking out might hurt their career," Barkley said in his *SNL* monologue. "Well, here's something that contradicts all of that: Me. I've been saying whatever the hell I want for over 30 years and I'm doing great … LeBron, keep on dribbling and don't ever shut up."

The audience cheered. And therein lies the difference in athlete activism today. Athletes have always spoken out on societal issues— Ali's anti-Vietnam stand in the '60s is oft-mentioned, but you could go all the way back to Irish long-jumper Peter O'Connor, an activist for Ireland's independence, waving the Irish flag when the British anthem played during the medal ceremony at the

1906 Olympic games. But few cheered. Ali, in fact, wasn't widely beloved in opinion polls until—not coincidentally—Parkinson's disease had robbed him of his voice.

"There have always been instances of social protest by athletes," says Dr. Douglas Hartmann, chair of the sociology department at the University of Minnesota and author of *Midnight Basketball: Race, Sports and Neoliberal Social Policy*. "But now it's a movement, and it's not just professional athletes."

Since at least 2012, it's become hard to pick up a sports page and not read about an athlete taking action or weighing in on life beyond his or her field of play. Name the issue and there's been an athlete, or group of athletes, engaging it: Racism, police brutality, gay and transgender rights. Others—Bob Knight, Curt Schilling—have stood for conservative causes.

What was once verboten has become trendy, and that's brought along its own backlash, as the NFL has found out. Last season, league TV ratings were down 10 percent and at least one study found that nearly one-third of 1,000 random respondents said they were less likely to watch a game because of players protesting during the national anthem. But that hasn't slowed the parade of athletes who are wading into societal matters.

What explains the trend? "It's a lot easier to feel free enough to get involved and take stands when the greatest athlete in the world leads the way," said Los Angeles Ram Connor Barwin, whose foundation rebuilds inner-city parks and who has supported political candidates, of LeBron James. James, who, in addition to dust-ups like the one with Ingraham, has underwritten some $40 million in college tuition for underprivileged children in his hometown of Akron, Ohio.

In the past, athletes like Ali who took socially impactful stands were isolated and shunned. Barkley says his outspokenness in the prime of his career cost him $10 million in endorsements and subjected him to criticism from the front office of his team, his league and the media. Controversial stands taken by NBA players Craig Hodges and Mahmoud Abdul-Rauf—whose protest over the national anthem presaged Colin Kaepernick's—resulted in the end of their careers, respectively. When Tommie Smith and John Carlos raised their fists during the medal ceremony in a Black Power salute at the 1968 Olympics, Brent Musburger referred to them on-air as "black-skinned stormtroopers" to nary a complaint.

What's changed? In recent years, Kaepernick's blackballing notwithstanding, establishment forces—perhaps kicking and screaming—have come to endorse, or at least grin and bear, athlete activism. Last fall, team owners lined up with NFL players taking a knee, defying President Trump; in response to campus racism, a boycott on football activities by the University of Missouri football team, supported by its coach, forced the resignation of the school's president; and the Miami Heat organization stood by James and his then-teammates when they tweeted a photo of themselves wearing hoodies with the hashtag #WeAreTrayvonMartin.

Establishment forces like teams, leagues and mass media outlets have come to realize the power and popularity of today's athletes and, perhaps calculatingly, have come to be on board with athletes who flex their social justice muscle. Ironically, the backlash now increasingly comes from the anti-establishment, nativist fringe.

"Don't underestimate the Trump effect," says Hartmann. "In the past, presidents have used sports to unify the country. When, last fall, Trump attacked primarily African-American football players who were protesting police brutality, he used politically motivated, racially coded speech to mobilize a nativist, reactionary response."

In that sense, Hartmann says, unlike in past examples of athlete protest, in this case the athletes were responding to, rather than making, a provocative message. Which gets us to that other hulking linebacker in the room: Race.

"There is and has always been a societal backlash against athletes, particularly Black athletes, who speak out against injustice," says Dr. Peter Kaufman, professor of sociology at the State University of New York at New Paltz, and author of "Boos, Bans, and Other Backlash: The Consequences of Being An Activist Athlete." "As William Rhoden wrote in his aptly titled book, many people view, although they would never admit or be even be conscious of, Black athletes as *40 Million Dollar Slaves*. Just shut up and play, entertain us. That's what we pay you for."

That's the resentment the likes of Trump and Ingraham have instinctively sought to exploit for political purposes. The same bitterness exists for celebrities as a whole who speak out, but it's easier to mobilize it by using African-American athletes. "First, there's long been this ideology of sport as apolitical," says Hartmann. "The separation of sports and politics has long been enshrined in Olympic ceremony and protocol, and a different standard has applied to, say, actors and actresses. So athletes who speak out have been up against that norm. But when Laura Ingraham calls LeBron's comments 'ungrammatical' she's also playing off dumb jock stereotypes unique to the athlete, especially the African-American."

But what the opponents haven't counted on is the media savviness of today's athlete. In the past, activists like Ali and Jim Brown were not only dependent on the often skewed filter of sportswriters, who were themselves saddled with biases, but also on a comparatively slow news cycle. Ali, for example, might be called a "draft dodger" and the defamatory claim would have the airwaves and newspaper pages to itself for days. Today, James and his colleagues are able to respond in real time to their critics, often capturing the high ground right away.

"For better or worse, social media has changed the landscape, particularly when it comes to social justice movements," says Kaufman. "Studies have shown that the World Trade Organization protests in Seattle in 1999 were driven by social media in a game-changing way. Fast forward to today, when our lives are structured around hashtags and soundbites. Social media has been a powerful tool to bring about solidarity, so an athlete who speaks out never has to really be all alone out there."

So there was James last fall, stealing the headline from Trump, the master headline maker, after the president preemptively withdrew a White House invitation to the NBA champion Golden

State Warriors after that team's star, Steph Curry, expressed his desire to skip the traditional visit. "U bum," James tweeted. "@StephenCurry30 already said he ain't going! So therefore ain't no invite. Going to White House was a great honor until you showed up!" The flurry of Twitter support for Curry, led by James, bore out Kaufman's point: The protester no longer has to go it alone. And it showed that athletes—with their millions of followers—could own the public narrative instead of finding themselves at its mercy.

It's a power trickling down to athletes who don't have the freedom that comes with million-dollar contracts. "In recent years, college athletes have publicly taken up the causes of racial justice and student-athlete rights, while still playing," says Dr. Victoria Jackson, a sports historian at Arizona State University. "They've been inspired by role models like LeBron James and Colin Kaepernick."

Jackson cites jocks turned change agents like Kain Colter, the quarterback who led the ultimately unsuccessful movement to unionize his team; Oklahoma's Eric Striker, who spoke out when a racist fraternity video came to light on his campus, and who engaged the "shut up and play" backlash in the pages of *Sports Illustrated*: "As a young man I thought, I'm gonna change the world, but I didn't know how. Now I have a platform and a voice people want to hear. Why would I stop talking?"; and Nigel Hayes, who, as a University of Wisconsin basketball star, called attention to NCAA exploitation by carrying a sign that read "Broke College Athlete Anything Helps" and who wrote a public letter critiquing his university on race relations: "We shouldn't be commodified for mere entertainment, but respected as individuals with the ideas and the ability to contribute to society."

There are those athletes who will likely never show up on *Sportscenter*. Hartmann cities the case of Olivia House, a sophomore soccer player at Division III Augsburg University in Minneapolis, who knelt during the anthem before her games last season after seeing Megan Rapinoe of the US women's national team do the same. "The parents of some of her teammates were upset, and they spoke to their kids, and that led to conversations within families and on the team about real issues," says Hartmann. "It didn't change the system, but it created awareness and started a dialogue."

Which is, after all, what movements do. The more athletes at all levels feel emboldened to make their voices heard on a wide range of issues, the likelier it is that the days of "Republicans buy sneakers, too" will be in our cultural rear view mirror. Some have called that Jordan quote apocryphal, but I asked him in the pages of *GQ* magazine in 2007 if he regretted it and he said: "No, I privately supported [the challenger to Senator Jesse Helms] Harvey Gantt … But if you asked me the pros and cons of Harvey Gantt, I'd have been lying to say one thing … I'd only be setting myself up for someone to scrutinize my opinions, which were limited, because I never channeled much energy into it."

Though he has been pilloried for the comment, in this explanation Jordan makes a compelling point: The call for athletes to speak out just might be a type of media set-up. Which is why today's generation of athlete activists have taken the work ethic they practiced in their sport and applied it to their activism. Two years ago, Malcolm Jenkins, the All-Pro safety for the Super Bowl champion Philadelphia Eagles was, like Jordan, focused on excelling in his sport. But then he saw the news reports of the killings by police of Philando Castile in Minnesota and Alton Sterling in Louisiana.

"I thought, 'That could have been me, or my brothers, or my cousins, or one of the kids my foundation serves,'" he says. "I looked at myself in the mirror and asked, am I doing enough?"

So he got to work. He read *The New Jim Crow* by Michelle Alexander, was transfixed by Ava DuVernay's 2016 documentary *13th*, interviewed inmates and the formerly incarcerated, picked the brains of community leaders, and went on ride-alongs with the police in Philadelphia's most dangerous neighborhoods. Jenkins decided he wasn't just going to symbolically protest; he was also going to advocate for substantive criminal justice reform.

When, last season, Jenkins' teammate Chris Long, who is white, put his arm around Jenkins during his raised fist national anthem protest, and when the two lobbied state officials together in support of a Clean Slate Bill that would seal old, non-violent misdemeanor offenses so those re-entering the work force could better find meaningful employment, it sent an important message: "Civil rights and criminal justice reform is not a black or white issue. It's an *American* issue," Jenkins says.

The backlash, Jenkins reports, has been minimal. In part, that's because he was savvy enough to understand what Jordan was getting at: He made himself an expert on a public policy issue. Of course, winning has also likely contributed to the resonance of his message.

But Jenkins is politically astute enough to know that, when the backlash comes, it's usually in the form of: *You're a millionaire athlete, what do you have to complain about? Shut up and play!* Like so many others of today's athlete activists, Jenkins flips that script, and argues that to whom much is given, even more is required. We have a patriotic duty to use our platform to better society, he says. And, somewhere up there, Ali is shuffling in celebration.

2

Athlete Activism Has a Long History

Brandon Tensley

Brandon Tensley is a contributing writer at Pacific Standard. *He is also an associate editor at* New America *and a co-host of* Slate's *"Outward" podcast.*

In this review of Howard Bryant's book, The Heritage: Black Athletes, a Divided America, and the Politics of Patriotism, *Brandon Tensley writes of the long history of athlete activism, whose latest avatar is LeBron James. Athletes, particularly black athletes, have often found themselves in a bind: they can either embrace activism or reject it in the interest of self-preservation. Athletes have historically paid a high price for speaking out. Former NFL star, singer, and actor Paul Robeson is but one example of a black celebrity who lost his livelihood after criticizing the status quo. Athletes such as O.J. Simpson, Michael Jordan, and Tiger Woods have been content to find their power in money as opposed to politics, a phenomenon that Howard Bryant calls "greenwashing." Bryant traces the re-emergence of black activism to 9/11, after which the police were lionized by the American public. African-Americans often saw another, more brutal side of the police, and thus athletes such as Colin Kaepernick were spurred to action.*

It was spectacular," the Cleveland Cavaliers' LeBron James said to a reporter in 2014. "I loved it. I'm looking for one." What could the hoops legend and multimillionaire possibly have wanted

"The Long, Defiant History of Activism Among Black Athletes," by Brandon Tensley, The Social Justice Foundation, June 8, 2018. Reprinted with permission of *Pacific Standard*.

that he didn't already own? Simple: a black T-shirt. Specifically, a black T-shirt with the phrase "I can't breathe" printed across the front. James had earlier seen Derrick Rose, then of the Chicago Bulls, wearing that shirt. In recent years, its message has become a rallying cry against police violence: In July of 2014, Eric Garner, an unarmed black man, died on Staten Island, New York, after police officers wrestled him into a deadly chokehold. According to a cell phone video, Garner's last words, which he repeated nearly a dozen times, were: "I can't breathe."

After some scrambling—and with an assist from Jay-Z—James secured the shirt in a day, just in time to wear it during warm-ups before a game against the Brooklyn Nets. Members of the British royal family also were in attendance that night. Through his hardwood attire, James was looking to issue his own salvo, to join a wave of national protest against the police brutality that has long plagued black American communities, but that too seldom earns more than a slap on the wrist, if that.

There's a term for someone like James, and increasingly it feels incendiary: athlete-activist. Why does the term feel incendiary? Because the political actions of the athlete-activist, especially if that person is black, tend to discomfit white viewers used to complacency. This kind of overt politics challenges the notion that an athlete's only job is to shut up and play.

With his world-historical fame, "King James" is a highly visible avatar of the athlete-activist, but he's also the latest entry in a much broader history. It's this lineage that the journalist Howard Bryant explores in his new book, *The Heritage: Black Athletes, a Divided America, and the Politics of Patriotism*. In particular, Bryant looks at how black athletes have found themselves in a political bind since World War II: Embrace politics, or keep it at arm's length in the interest of self-preservation.

Bryant traces the birth of this modern black political-athletic heritage, a concept he simply calls "the Heritage," to Paul Robeson. At the Paris Peace Conference in 1949, the former NFL star and bass-baritone singer delivered a seminal condemnation of

American racism, while noting the Soviet Union's more enlightened official stance on integration: "Why should the Negroes ever fight against the only nations of the world where racial discrimination is prohibited, and where the people can live freely?" Robeson asked. "Never! I can assure you, they will never fight against either the Soviet Union or the peoples' democracies." Reeling, McCarthy-era America deployed the celestial baseball player Jackie Robinson to dismiss Robeson, a.k.a. the "Bad Negro," as Bryant frames it. In his testimony before the House Un-American Activities Committee, Robinson said that Robeson's statement "sounds very silly." He added: "I've got too much invested for my wife and child and myself in the future of this country ... to throw it away because of a siren song sung in bass." This blistering repudiation helped contribute to Robeson's ruin: financial hardship, the loss of his passport, and harassment by the government.

But Robinson was arguably playing a longer game. As Bryant points out, within Robinson's testimony before HUAC "were the seeds of ... the radical Robinson who never backed down," who criticized the hypocrisy of a mealy mouthed America that wanted to denounce the illiberalism of communist countries while failing to address its own racist regime. "Negroes were stirred up long before there was a Communist Party, and they'll stay stirred up long after the party has disappeared—unless Jim Crow has disappeared by then as well," Robinson told HUAC.

For some 20-plus years, the Heritage thrived, sustained by figures like Cassius Clay and Lew Alcindor, both of whom later converted to Islam and officially change their names—to Muhammad Ali and Kareem Abdul-Jabbar, respectively. Nodding to his pan-African beliefs, Ali remarked in a 1975 *Playboy* interview: "Sure, I know I got it made while the masses of black people are catchin' hell, but as long as they ain't free, I ain't free."

Then O.J. Simpson came along.

One of the sharpest, most interesting facets of Bryant's analysis is his interrogation of "greenwashing," which is Bryant's term for the decision by some black athletes to seek power through cash, rather than through political action: "Instead of athletes using their celebrity to advocate for black people, as the old guard had, elite black players now opted for big salaries to sell sports and products, to help white America believe that all the messy history—and the nagging realities of the present—was gone."

To an extent, it became increasingly tempting to take this approach to athleticism: With the rise of endorsement deals, the allure of securing wealth essentially helped foreclose meaningful political action. Moreover, the sociologist and civil rights activist Harry Edwards tells Bryant that "the seminal issue from about 1975 to 2010 … was the absence of a defining ideology and movement that would frame and inform activist positions." Likewise, Simpson focused not on advocacy but on ads—endorsing everything from orange juice (naturally) to Hertz rent-a-cars. As he once (in)famously said: "I'm not black. I'm O.J." But it wasn't just Simpson; throughout the rest of the 20th century, athletic phenoms such as Michael Jordan and Tiger Woods, too, were skittish around politics. Bryant argues that greenwashing effectively killed the Heritage, or at least put it on life support.

To understand what fueled the re-emergence of the black athlete-activist of today, Bryant argues, it's necessary to look at the profound effects that 9/11 had on American culture. In the aftermath of the attacks, which claimed the lives of more than 400 emergency workers in addition to nearly 3,000 civilians, "the police-as-hero narrative appeared, stuck, remained, persisted, and spread," he writes. Within years, this largely uncritical embrace of law enforcement ran up against the growing visibility of police brutality, exemplified by the deaths of Michael Brown, Tamir Rice, and Sandra Bland, among others. Bryant argues that the "runaway 9/11 narrative of police pageantry did not square with the daily experience of how law enforcement dealt with black people." Today, this tension is perhaps most noticeable in the struggle of Colin Kaepernick, the former quarterback for the San Francisco 49ers. Since 2016, Kaepernick's decision to sit and later kneel during the national anthem, as a form of silent protest against racial injustice, has become a lightning rod for the fury of the American right.

Yet the real value of *The Heritage* lies in Bryant's awareness of just how long this has all been going on. At a time when it's easy to lose sight of the historical context of the black athlete-activist, who today is often wealthy beyond imagination, Bryant keeps his eye on the ball. His investigation helps readers see the arc from mid-century politics to, say, Serena Williams, whose prodigious tennis career hasn't shielded her from feeling compelled to take political actions mirroring those of her forerunners, such as speaking publicly against police violence. On top of that, Bryant writes with the kind of vim, in turns darkly comic and serious, that pulls you from page to page. It's a bracing analysis that brings clarity during a hazy season of "kneeling and blacklisting, of patriotism and heroes, some real, many more contrived."

3

Jesse Owens Refuted Hitler's Beliefs in the 1936 Olympics

Lawrence W. Reed

Lawrence W. Reed is president emeritus and Humphreys Family Senior Fellow at the Foundation for Economic Education and author of Real Heroes: Inspiring True Stories of Courage, Character, and Conviction *and* Excuse Me, Professor: Challenging the Myths of Progressivism.

In 1936, Adolf Hitler sought to use the Olympics in Berlin to further Nazi propaganda and his myth of Aryan supremacy. But African American track superstar Jesse Owens had other ideas. In winning four gold medals in front of Hitler, Owens provided irrefutable visual proof that Hitler's ideology was suspect. Owens even befriended Luz Long, the German long jump champion he defeated, and the pair walked the running track arm-in-arm in a show of human solidarity. But Owens said worse than Hitler was being snubbed by his own president and country upon his return.

James Cleveland "Jesse" Owens famously won four gold medals, all at the 1936 games in Berlin, Germany. But in the hearts of Americans who know their Olympic history, this African American man did more than win races: he struggled against racism.

"Jesse Owens: 'Character Makes the Difference When It's Close,'" by Lawrence W. Reed, Foundation for Economic Education, August 21, 2015. https://fee.org/articles/hitler-didn-t-snub-me-it-was-our-president/. Licensed under CC-BY 4.0 International. This essay appeared as a chapter in Mr. Reed's book, *Real Heroes: Inspiring True Stories of Courage, Character and Conviction*.

At the time of Owens's death in 1980 at age 66, President Jimmy Carter paid this tribute to him:

> *Perhaps no athlete better symbolized the human struggle against tyranny, poverty, and racial bigotry. His personal triumphs as a world-class athlete and record holder were the prelude to a career devoted to helping others. His work with young athletes, as an unofficial ambassador overseas, and a spokesman for freedom are a rich legacy to his fellow Americans.*

Carter's words were especially fitting in light of an unfortunate fact in Owens's life: unforgivably, a previous American president had given him the brush-off.

Born in Alabama in 1913, James Owens at the age of nine moved with his family to the town in Ohio that bore his middle name, Cleveland. His first school teacher there asked him his name. With a deep Southern twang, he replied "J.C. Owens." She heard "Jesse," so that's what she wrote down. The name stuck for the next 57 years.

Jesse could run like the wind and jump like a kangaroo. He broke junior high school records in the high jump and the broad jump. In high school, he won every major track event in which he competed, tying or breaking world records in the 100-yard and 220-yard dashes and setting a new world record in the broad jump. Universities showered him with scholarship offers, but he turned them all down and chose Ohio State, which wasn't extending track scholarships at the time.

Imagine it. You come from a relatively poor family. You could go to any number of colleges for next to nothing, but you pick one you have to pay for. At 21, you have a wife to support as well. So what do you do? If you are Jesse Owens, you work your way through school as a gas station attendant, a waiter, an all-night elevator operator, a library assistant, even a page in the Ohio legislature. Owens worked, studied, practiced on the field, and set more records in track during his years at OSU.

The biography at JesseOwens.com tells the stunning story that unfolded in 1935:

Jesse gave the world a preview of things to come in Berlin while at the Big Ten Championships in Ann Arbor on May 25, 1935, [where] he set three world records and tied a fourth, all in a span of about 45 minutes. Jesse was uncertain as to whether he would be able to participate at all, as he was suffering from a sore back as a result of a fall down a flight of stairs. He convinced his coach to allow him to run the 100-yard dash as a test for his back, and amazingly he recorded an official time of 9.4 seconds, once again tying the world record. Despite the pain, he then went on to participate in three other events, setting a world record in each event. In a span of 45 minutes, Jesse accomplished what many experts still feel is the greatest athletic feat in history—setting three world records and tying a fourth in four grueling track and field events.

Ohio wasn't the Deep South, but in the mid-1930s, it wasn't a paradise of racial equality, either. OSU required Owens and other black athletes to live together off campus. They had to order carryout or eat at "black-only" restaurants and stay in segregated hotels when traveling with the team.

The eyes of the world were focused on Berlin in early August 1936. Five years earlier and before the Nazis came to power, the German capital had been selected as the site for the summer 1936 Olympic games. An effort to boycott them because of Hitler's racism fizzled. It would be a few more years before events convinced the world of the socialist dictator's evil intentions. Jesse Owens entered the competition with Americans thrilled at his prospects but wondering how Hitler would react if "Aryan superiority" fell short of his expectations.

Jesse didn't go to Berlin with a political axe to grind. "I wanted no part of politics," he said. "And I wasn't in Berlin to compete against any one athlete. The purpose of the Olympics, anyway, was to do your best. As I'd learned long ago … the only victory that counts is the one over yourself."

If, a hundred years from now, only one name is remembered among those who competed at the Berlin games, it will surely be that of Jesse Owens.

Owens won the 100-meter sprint, the long jump, the 200-meter sprint, and the 4 x 100 sprint relay. In the process, he became the first American to claim four gold medals in a single Olympiad. Owens waved at Hitler and Hitler waved back, but the nasty little paper-hanger expressed his annoyance privately to fellow Nazi Albert Speer. He opined that blacks should never be allowed to compete in the games again.

A side story of Owens's Berlin experience was the friendship he made with a German competitor named Luz Long. A decent man by any measure, Long exhibited no racial animosity and even offered tips to Owens that the American found helpful during the games. Of Long, Owens would later tell an interviewer,

> It took a lot of courage for him to befriend me in front of Hitler … You can melt down all the medals and cups I have and they wouldn't be a plating on the 24-karat friendship I felt for Lutz Long at that moment. Hitler must have gone crazy watching us embrace. The sad part of the story is I never saw Long again. He was killed in World War II.

Back home, ticker tape parades feted Owens in New York City and Cleveland. Hundreds of thousands of Americans came out to cheer him. Letters, phone calls, and telegrams streamed in from around the world to congratulate him. From one important man, however, no word of recognition ever came. As Owens later put it, "Hitler didn't snub me; it was our president who snubbed me. The president didn't even send a telegram."

Franklin Delano Roosevelt, leader of a major political party with deep roots in racism, couldn't bring himself to utter a word of support, which may have been a factor in Owens's decision to campaign for Republican Alf Landon in the 1936 presidential election. FDR invited all the white US Olympians to the White House, but not Jesse.

"It all goes so fast, and character makes the difference when it's close," Owens once said about athletic competition. He could have taught FDR a few lessons in character, but the president never gave him the chance. Owens wouldn't be invited to the White House for almost 20 years—not until Dwight Eisenhower named him "Ambassador of Sports" in 1955.

Life after the Olympics wasn't always kind to Jesse Owens. When he wanted to earn money from commercial endorsements, athletic officials yanked his amateur status. Then the commercial offers dried up. He was forced to file for bankruptcy. He felt the sting of racial discrimination again. But for the last 30 years of his life, until he died in 1980 of lung cancer, he found helping underprivileged teenagers to be even more personally satisfying than his Olympic gold medals.

4

Tommie Smith and John Carlos Paid a High Price for Their Activism

Jules Boykoff

Jules Boykoff is a professor of politics and government at Pacific University in Forest Grove, Oregon. His books include Activism and the Olympics; Celebration Capitalism and the Olympic Games; Landscapes of Dissent; *and* Beyond Bullets: The Suppression of Dissent in the United States.

At the 1968 Olympics in Mexico, sprinters Tommie Smith and John Carlos raised their black-gloved fists during the national anthem as they stood on the victory stand. They were protesting the poverty and racism that plagued the United States and the world at large. It was a protest that reverberated around the world and made those in power nervous because they believed politics had no place in the Olympics. Smith and Carlos were subsequently punished for their actions. They were sent home from the Olympics prematurely, and their athletic careers suffered. But Smith, Carlos, and Australian sprinter Peter Norman, who stood with them in solidarity, never backtracked on their position, and history has vindicated them.

Anti-apartheid activism created momentum for a historic act of dissent on a related but separate issue. At the 1968 Summer Games in Mexico City, the African American track stars Tommie Smith and John Carlos stood in their socks on the medal stand and

"Tommie Smith, John Carlos, and the 1968 Olympics: 50 Years Later," by Jules Boykoff, Verso Books, October 16, 2018. Reprinted by permission.

thrust their black-glove-clad fists toward the sky as they bowed their heads while the US national anthem played. They were protesting the poverty and racism that plagued the United States and the wider world. Their shoeless feet and black socks symbolized poverty. Their black gloves signified black pride. Carlos's open jacket represented his working-class roots. Carlos later wrote: "We decided that we would wear black gloves to represent strength and unity. We would have beads hanging from our neck, which would represent the history of lynching. We wouldn't wear shoes to symbolize the poverty that still plagued so much of black America. On the medal stand, all we would wear on our feet would be black socks." As Tommie Smith later explained, "The totality of our effort was the regaining of our black dignity." Carlos told me they took action "to set a standard. To have a society show its best face. To bring attention to the plight of people who were less fortunate. To wake up the consciousness of those who had let their conscience go dormant. And to encourage people to stand for what's right as opposed to standing for nothing." Both men pinned human-rights buttons on their track jackets. The silver medalist, Peter Norman of Australia, sported a button in solidarity.

Radical politics were thrumming around the globe as the Olympics took the stage in Mexico City, and so was the violent reaction of the state. Only a few weeks prior at Tlatelolco Plaza in the host city, security forces massacred scores, perhaps hundreds of protesters, a measure of how far Mexican authorities were willing to go to maintain order. The Tlatelolco Plaza demonstrators were protesting the allocation of vast funds for the Olympics while social programs went unfunded. [IOC chairman Avery] Brundage took stock of the turbulent times and told the opening session of the IOC, "We live today in an uneasy and even rebellious world, a world marked by injus-tice, aggression, demonstrations, disorder, turmoil, violence and war, against which all civilized persons rebel, but this is no reason to destroy the nucleus of international cooperation and goodwill we have created in the Olympic Movement." Trying to distance the Olympic movement from the radical politics of the moment, he added, "You don't find hippies, yippies or beatniks on sports grounds."

But there were principled activist-athletes on the playing fields of 1968. Smith and Carlos were not lone renegades; they were part of a political movement rooted in athletic achievement. In the United States, Harry Edwards, a sociologist and political organizer, had helped found the Olympic Project for Human Rights (OPHR) in 1967. At a press conference in December of that year, the group unveiled six demands, which it listed as following:

> *Restoration of Muhammad Ali's title and right to box in this country.*
>
> *Removal of the anti-Semitic and anti-black personality Avery Brundage from his post as Chairman of the International Olympic Committee.*
>
> *Curtailment of participation of all-white teams and individuals from the Union of South Africa and Southern Rhodesia in all United States Olympic Athletic events.*
>
> *The addition of at least two black coaches to the men's track and field coaching staff appointed to coach the 1968 United States Olympic team.*
>
> *The appointment of at least two black people to policy-making positions on the United States Olympic Committee.*
>
> *The complete desegregation of the bigot-dominated and racist New York Athletic Club.*

The IOC president and the injustices emanating from South Africa sat in the center of OPHR's sites, evidence of the group's global vision. Tommie Smith stressed in his autobiography that the OPHR's name highlighted "human rights, not civil rights—nothing to do with the Panthers or Black Power—all humanity, even those who denied us ours." Yet improving the lives of black people was a central goal. Writing retrospectively, Edwards identified OPHR's key aims: "to stage an international protest of the persistent and systematic violation of black people's human rights in the United States" and "to expose America's historical exploitation of black athletes as political propaganda tools in both the national and international arenas."

To press toward these goals, the OPHR threatened to orchestrate a boycott of the 1968 Games. In April, to combat apartheid, sixty-five US athletes signed on to a list that supported a boycott if South Africa were allowed to participate. Numerous prominent athletes signed, including Arthur Ashe, Wilt Chamberlain, Jim Bouton, Len Wilkins, Oscar Robertson, Jackie Robinson, and Ruben Amaro. The track stars John Carlos and Lee Evans also joined. A few months earlier, Jackie Robinson led a group of famous athletes, including Tommie Smith, Dave Bing, Bob Gibson and K. C. Jones, pushing for South Africa to be banned from the Games. Months of activist campaigning—often led by athletes themselves—built up to Smith and Carlos's act of defiance. Movements created space for the athletes' iconic moment.

Meanwhile, the powerful were becoming nervous. In July 1968, Vincent X. Flaherty, a Los Angeles sports journalist, wrote Brundage a letter that promised to craft a critical article on the boycott threat. Flaherty asked: "Why can't the Negro athletes sign now as to their intentions? Why can't recalitrants [sic] be barred now so as to avoid any possible disgraceful demonstrations[?]" Ditching even the pretense of journalistic objectivity, he also suggested ignoring OPHR figure Harry Edwards: "I think this man Edward's [sic] name should be kept out of print, and I also think the IOC should take a definitive action." He added, "I think you will agree this sort of thing has no place in the Olympics as a whole, nor does it have any right to be foisted upon the host country." Indeed the IOC president agreed. In less than two weeks Brundage responded: "The action of Edwards is directed against the people of the United States ... It is unfortunate that so much publicity is given to these people." He continued, "The Olympic Games have given the negro an opportunity to display his talents on a completely equal basis, and it is outrageous that they should be used for political purposes." This interaction underlines what sociologist Ben Carrington calls "the fear of the black athlete" as rooted in "the projection of white masculinist fantasies of domination [and] control." The powerful were squirming.

The sports media establishment tended to agree with the Brundage line, urging the athletes to shut up and play. Once Smith and Carlos took their stand on the medal stand, many commentators became outright hostile. Arthur Daley of the *New York Times* wrote, "Smith and Carlos brought their world smack into the Olympic Games, where it did not belong, and created a shattering situation that shook this international sports carnival to its very core. They were also divisive." Brent Musburger, writing for the *Chicago American*, railed against the "black-skinned storm troopers" he deemed "unimaginative blokes." He fumed: "One gets a little tired of having the United States run down by athletes who are enjoying themselves at the expense of their country. Protesting and working constructively against racism in the United States is one thing, but airing one's dirty clothing before the entire world during a fun-and-games tournament was no more than a juvenile gesture by a couple of athletes who should have known better." The *New York Times* found division within the US squad. The gold-medal-winning boxer George Foreman, who dismissed their efforts, told the paper: "That's for college kids. They live in another world."

Brundage was livid with Smith and Carlos. He pressured the US Olympic Committee to suspend the athletes from the team and dismiss them from the Olympic Village. The USOC obliged, releasing a statement that read in part, "The United States Olympic Committee expresses its profound regrets to the International Olympic Committee, to the Mexican Organizing Committee and to the people of Mexico for the discourtesy displayed by two members of its team in departing from tradition during a victory ceremony at the Olympic Stadium on October 16th." The USOC labeled their act "untypical exhibitionism" that "violates the basic standards of sportsmanship and good manners." Pivoting to threat, it then noted, "A repetition of such incidents by other members of the US team can only be considered a willful disregard of Olympic principles that would warrant the severest penal-ties." This threat was echoed by the IOC official Lord David Burghley—also known as the Marquess of Exeter—who said: "I will not countenance such actions again. I'll refuse to hold a victory ceremony if any such attempt is made again."

Brundage received a trailer load of mail regarding the Smith and Carlos affair and how he handled it. Many defended the act of dissent. One letter writer told Brundage, "A wonderful week of sportsmanship has been spoiled for me by the punishment of the young American athletes," and added, "these young men understood that justice and brotherhood are the only gold medal worth having, and they had the courage to stand up and say so." Another alluded to South Africa's exclusion from the Games and asked: "Yet two Negro athletes were expelled for 'mixing politics and athletics.' How hypocritical can you get?!" One critic from Los Angeles slammed "the senseless, idiotic, racist reaction of our Olympic Committee." He concluded that Carlos and Smith "will be greeted as black power heroes by an incensed black America, more convinced than ever that white America has nothing but hatred for the black man." He closed by promising to send a $25 check to the Urban League "in the hopes that they can achieve brotherhood in the world, since you have so badly failed."

Numerous people writing Brundage specified that they were white before accusing the International Olympic Committee of undermining "one of the United States' most cherished traditions, the right to speak out" and taking action that was "disgusting, uncalled for, narrow-minded, and indicative of your prejudice." Many called the suspension of Smith and Carlos "unduly harsh treatment for their quiet and dignified act of protest against conditions in their country. They were not protesting the Olympic Committee, or the games, or Mexico, or any other country." Telegrams flooded in from around the world from groups like the Athletex Welfare Association of Nigeria and the Southern Christian Leadership Conference (SCLC). Jesse Jackson wrote a telegram directly to Tommie Smith congratulating him for his courageous act, stating, "You may have been on the wrong side of the Olympic Committee, but on the right side of history." He issued Smith an open invitation to come speak at the SCLC's breadbasket community meetings, expenses paid.

Many, however, weighed in to chastise Carlos and Smith and offer support to Brundage. Racism sometimes showed through, as in a letter from Omaha, Nebraska, that read:

> *The actions of the two Negroes, Smith and Carlos, was a national disgrace. I hope you stick to your decision to keep them off the team. Some others should be booted off, too. Our State Dept. should take action on such traitors, but for political expediency they won't. The white man owes the Negro nothing. Let some of them return to the stone age delights of tribal Africa. In all time the Negro race is the only race to have contributed nothing toward civilization. They do excell [sic] in motor co-ordination.*

Brundage often took the time to respond to letter writers who supported the dismissal of Smith and Carlos. Frequently he wrote, "Good manners and sportsmanship are more important than athletic ability." Among the other sentiments he expressed: "We do not propose to permit demonstrations of any kind at the Olympic Games"; "The boys were sent home, but they should not have been there in the first place"; "As a matter of fact people of that kind should not have been on the Olympic team at all. This was not a school boy prank as some seem to think … it left international repercussions very harmful to our country"; "You are exactly right and your views have been supported by all true United States citizens. The action of these negroes was an insult to the Mexican hosts and a disgrace to the United States."

After the Games, Brundage bristled over the possible inclusion of Smith and Carlos in the official Olympic film. In a letter to the chair of the Mexico City Organizing Committee, Brundage railed about "the rumors that have reached my ears about the use of pictures of the nasty demonstration against the United States flag by negroes in the official film of the Games of the XIX Olympiad." He went on to argue, "It had nothing to do with sport, it was a shameful abuse of hospitality and it has no more place in the record of the Games than the gunfire at Tlatelolco." He reiterated his point by concluding, "With the hope that this objectionable feature will be eliminated, I am." In a separate letter, Mexican IOC member José de J. Clark wrote, "To beg you that said scene be omitted from the official film of the Olympic Games." The Mexico City Olympic organizers wrote back with a compromise: excluding the protest by Smith and Carlos in the version of the film sent to the official IOC archive and to NOCs, but keeping it in the copies that would be shown commercially. Brundage's biographer notes: "Brundage was clearly unable in this instance to apply the aesthetic criteria that he relied upon in his eloquent defense of Leni Riefenstahl's film of the 1936 games. The Nazi salute and the swastika were part of the Gesamtkunstwerk of the Olympic ceremony, but the black-power salute and the black berets were somehow 'political.'"

Both Carlos and Smith paid a high price for their actions. They received a steady stream of threats on their lives. They were pilloried in the press. Jobs were scarce. They lost marriages to the stress. Carlos and Smith's own relationship strained as friction mounted between them. Peter Norman, who stood with them in solidarity on the medal stand, was treated like a pariah in Australia. Despite posting times that would qualify him for the 1972 Games, he was cut from the Australia squad. When Sydney hosted the 2000 Olympics, Norman was not officially acknowledged.

Yet Smith, Carlos, and Norman never backtracked, and history has vindicated them. Even President Barack Obama publicly praised Carlos and Smith. "To signify in that Olympics that there was more work to do, to acknowledge the injustices that were still taking place, I think that was a breakthrough moment in an overall push to move this country towards a more equal and more just society," he said, "I think that what they did was in the best tradition of American protest." This is an example of the common tendency to revere activists the further they recede in the rearview mirror of history. The entire episode also highlights, as the sociologist Douglas Hartmann puts it, "the thrill of victory and the agony of activism," and helps us understand why more Olympic athletes don't use their high-profile athletic stage to engage politics.

The athlete-activism did not end with Carlos and Smith. Vera Caslavska, the most successful Czech gymnast in the history of the Olympics, also took a political stand on the medal stand. Two months before the Mexico City Games commenced, the Soviet Union led an invasion of Czechoslovakia in order to crush the "Prague Spring," inklings of democracy—or at least moves toward less surveillance and repression—that aimed to loosen the Soviet stranglehold on the country. The Czechoslovak National Olympic Committee nearly opted to withdraw from the 1968 Games, as the incursion made training nearly impossible for athletes and major transatlantic airlines were not flying out of Prague. Less than a month before the Games' opening ceremony, Czechoslovakia decided to press ahead and send its 100-strong team to Mexico City.

Caslavska had already established herself as a top-flight gymnast, winning three gold medals and a silver at the Tokyo 1964 Olympics. She had also shown herself to be an athlete willing to speak out, signing onto the Manifesto of 2,000 Words in April 1968, which protested Soviet hegemony in Czechoslovakia. Four months later, the Soviets invaded and Caslavska fled into hiding where she trained in suboptimal, stressful conditions. But with the Soviet-led assault as a political backdrop, Caslavska shined in Mexico City, winning four more gold medals and two silvers. In the process, she beat out archrival Soviet gymnasts, to the ecstatic cheers of local spectators, and not simply because she selected the "Mexican Hat Dance" as the accompaniment for her final floor performance. Only days after Carlos and Smith thrust their fists skyward, Caslavska made her own political statement on the medal stand, if a more subtle one, dipping her head in silent protest during the Russian national anthem. Caslavska was clearly motivated by politics. "I am a Czechoslovak citizen," she later said. "We all tried harder to win in Mexico because it would turn the eyes of the world on our unfortunate country." She paid a price for her principles. The Soviet-compliant government in Prague forbade her from traveling abroad or from competing in gymnastics. But years later, with another significant shift in the political winds and the rise of Vaclav Havel, Caslavska would become the head of the Czech National Olympic Committee as well as the eighth woman coopted as a member of the IOC.

5

Muhammad Ali Rewrote the Rules of Athlete Activism

David Rowe

David Rowe is Professor of Cultural Research at the Institute for Culture and Society of Western Sydney University in Australia. His books include Sport, Culture and the Media: The Unruly Trinity, Global Media Sport: Flows, Forms and Futures *and* Sport Beyond Television: The Internet, Digital Media and the Rise of Networked Media Sport.

Many years before athletes began using social media to communicate directly with the world and polish their image, Muhammad Ali ruled the media with his unconventional publicity stunts, whacky poems, and catchy phrases. According to Rowe, Ali is in the conversation when it comes to the most-important athletes ever, not only because of his boxing prowess, but because he was willing to stand up to the establishment when it came to important social issues and lead the way for future athletes. When he refused to serve in Vietnam, he became a lightning rod for both hatred and hope in a deeply divided America. The sport that brought him to prominence is much maligned today due to the concerns about brain injuries, but Rowe believes that we should be grateful that this violent sport brought Ali to worldwide fame, enabling him to set a new standard for athlete activism.

The descriptor "icon" is vastly overused in these celebrity-fixated times, but it could have been invented for Muhammad Ali, who has died aged 74. Thirty-five years after he threw his last punch in the ring, Ali is still front of mind in any discussion of the most-important sportsman ever.

He does not occupy this status because he is widely regarded as the best boxer there has ever been, who narcissistically called himself "The Greatest," and then forced a reluctant boxing world to agree. Ali was much bigger than boxing. He came, from the late 1960s onwards, to symbolise resistance to racism, militarism and inequality.

He embodied the intimate relationship between sport and politics that so troubles those, like nationalistic politicians, who deny its existence while ruthlessly exploiting it.

So how did Ali so consistently receive the kind of acclaim heaped on him by human rights activist and sports scholar Richard E. Lapchick, who describes Ali as "not a one-in-a-million figure, but a once-in-a-lifetime person"?

Ali was a superlative boxer, but it was his great physical beauty and quick wit that made a major impression on those who knew little of boxing or were repelled by its brutality. Under his birth name, Cassius Clay, he forced himself into public consciousness by theatrically talking up his "prettiness," athletic brilliance and verbal facility.

From early in his career he self-consciously played the role of anti-hero with a racial twist. Knowing the white-dominated boxing establishment and fan base were always searching, especially in the prestigious heavyweight division, for a "great white hope" to put African-American champions in their place, Ali goaded them to find him another fighter to beat.

Decades before sportspeople used social media to communicate directly with the world and polish their image, Ali bent the media of the day to his will through outrageous publicity stunts, quirky poems and memorable catchphrases. Another white-dominated institution, the mainstream media, had to deal with an unprecedented, freewheeling assault on its familiar control routines by a black athlete who refused to be deferent and grateful.

This boxing-related pantomime was entertaining. But it was when the brand new world heavyweight champion rejected his "slave name" in 1964, became Muhammad Ali and declared his allegiance to the black separatist Nation of Islam that he became a major political presence in popular culture.

His subsequent refusal—on religious and ethical grounds—to be conscripted to the US armed forces and to fight in the Vietnam War turned him into both a figure of hate and a symbol of hope in a bitterly divided America. The world beyond boxing and America now had even more reason to pay close attention to Muhammad Ali.

Once more, Ali was ahead of the game. Anticipating the deep political divisions over the two Gulf Wars and their disastrous outcomes, here was a vibrant celebrity around whom dissenters could rally.

Banned from boxing for three years because of his political stance, Ali acquired the status of a martyr to his convictions. He stood conspicuous among fellow sport stars who kept their heads down on matters of politics—whatever their private views.

In retrospect, it is remarkable that he was not assassinated like the Kennedys, Martin Luther King Jr, and Malcolm X.

When he returned to the ring, Ali became the focus of spectacular media-sport events like "The Rumble in the Jungle" and "The Thrilla in Manila". These boxing matches helped write the rule book of 21st-century "sportainment."

Ali's boxing career petered out, yet he remained an instantly recognisable global celebrity. But by 1984 the savage toll that boxing took on his body, especially his brain, became evident. It is believed to have exacerbated the Parkinson's disease that progressively debilitated him.

Some of the most touching and heart-breaking moments in sport came when his shaking body performed ceremonial duties at the 1996 Atlanta and 2012 London Olympics. When Ali spoke in public, his rapid-fire repartee was reduced to a low, slow whisper.

Despite his failing health, Ali relentlessly pursued his humanistic activities. He supported charities and foundations such as Athletes for Hope, UNICEF, and his own Muhammad Ali Center.

Ali was no saint. His cruel mocking of rival Joe Frazier, which he later regretted, saw him treat a fellow African American as a "dumb," "ugly," racially complicit Uncle Tom in a manner that resonated with some of the worst racist stereotypes. His complicated history of intimate relationships with women and his many offspring is of soap-opera proportions.

But, in touching and enhancing the lives of so many people across the globe, here was a man much more sinned against than sinning.

Ali's passing comes at a time of increasing concern about sport-induced traumatic brain injury. The near-fatal outcome of a recent bout in the UK between Nick Blackwell and Chris Eubank Jr has once again put boxing in an unfavourable spotlight.

Ali paid a ferocious price for his fame. Most leading medical associations would ban the sport that brought him to prominence.

Yet, paradoxically, it is boxing that we have to thank for somehow—out of the violence and pain of its self-proclaimed "sweet science"—delivering to the world Muhammad Ali, The People's Champion.

6

Craig Hodges Spoke Out When His Teammate Michael Jordan Could Not

Donald McRae

Donald McRae is an award-winning South African writer. His many books include Dark Trade: Lost in Boxing *and* In Black and White: The Untold Story of Joe Louis and Jesse Owens.

While his teammate, superstar Michael Jordan, famously refused to take a political stance, Craig Hodges was never shy about voicing his views on society, particularly those about offenses committed against fellow African Americans. Hodges regrets that his generation of black athletes did not do more to address social inequities during his career, saying that athletes were too concerned with branding and not social justice. Hodges even attempted to convince Jordan to do more for black communities, but Jordan demurred. When the New York Times *ran a story in which Hodges spoke out against racism and criticized Jordan for failing to address the Rodney King beating, it effectively ended his NBA career. Like many other athletes, Hodges paid a dear price for his outspokenness.*

I'm sad to say that one of our players was shot on Monday," Craig Hodges reveals after he has spoken for an hour about his brave but tumultuous career in the NBA. Hodges fell out with Michael Jordan, confronted [George H. W. Bush] in the White

"Craig Hodges: 'Jordan Didn't Speak Out Because He Didn't Know What to Say,'" by Donald McRae, Guardian News and Media Limited, April 20, 2017. Reprinted by permission.

House and won two championships with his hometown team, at a time when the Chicago Bulls were venerated around the world, before he was ostracised and shut out of basketball for being too politically outspoken.

At home in Chicago, where Hodges and one of his sons, Jamaal, now coach basketball at his old high school, Rich East, his urgency is tinged with pathos. "He's in surgery right now," the 56-year-old says of his wounded player. "He got shot in the hip. He's only a freshman so he's just a 15-year-old. It's stuff like this we're battling every day. A few weekends ago in Chicago, five people got killed, so it's terrible. There is so much injustice, but it's just a matter of time before we win these battles."

Hodges has told his compelling life story with fiery passion, looping around a cast of characters stretching from Jordan, Magic Johnson and Phil Jackson back to Muhammad Ali, Arthur Ashe and Kareem Abdul-Jabbar, before returning to the present. Sport and politics are entwined again in a country where Donald Trump is president and Colin Kaepernick remains locked outside football as an unsigned free agent who had the temerity to sink to one knee during the national anthem. And teenage African American boys, just like they were when Hodges was trying to shake up the NBA, are still being gunned down.

Hodges always wanted to voice his opposition to injustice. In June 1991, before the first game of the NBA finals between the Bulls and the LA Lakers, Hodges tried to convince Jordan and Magic Johnson that both teams should stage a boycott. Rodney King, an African American, had been beaten brutally by four white policemen in Los Angeles three months earlier—while 32% of the black population in Illinois lived below the poverty line.

As he writes in his new book *Long Shot: The Triumphs and Struggles of an NBA Freedom Fighter*, Hodges told the sport's two leading players that the Bulls and Lakers should sit out the opening game, so "we would stand in solidarity with the black community while calling out racism and economic inequality in the NBA, where there were no black owners and almost no black coaches despite the fact that 75% of the players in the league were African American."

Jordan told Hodges he was "crazy" while Johnson said: "That's too extreme, man."

"What's happening to our people in this country is extreme," Hodges replied.

The finals were played as normal, and Hodges and the Bulls won the championship, but he regrets the failure to stage a united protest. "Our generation dropped the ball as a lot of us were more concerned with our own economic gain. We were at that point where branding was just beginning and we got caught up in individual branding rather than a unified movement."

Hodges became a one-man protest movement within the NBA. In October 1991, the Bulls were invited to the White House to meet President Bush. The assault on King remained fresh in his mind, as did the US bombing of Iraq that January, and so Hodges wrote an impassioned eight-page letter to the president—on behalf of "most specifically, the African Americans who are not able to come to this great edifice and meet the leader of the nation in which they live."

He wore a dashiki and George W, the president's son and a future occupant of the Oval Office, spoke slowly as if Hodges might not understand English. "Where are you from?"

"Chicago Heights, Illinois," Hodges answered, amused at the way in which W's excitement at meeting the famous Bulls, which had him "bouncing around like a kid" at his father's workplace, had disappeared into startled incomprehension.

Phil Jackson, the Bulls' coach, informed the president that Hodges was the Bulls' best shooter. On a half-court set up on the South Lawn, Hodges drained three-pointers from 24 feet. He hit nine in a row, his white dashiki swirling gently around him. As they left the court, Hodges told the president he had written him a personal letter.

Did Bush reply to the letter? "He never did," Hodges says, calmly. "I wonder sometimes if he got past page one. I wonder if he even read it? When I was researching my book I got in touch with the George Bush library to get the original copy. The lady there loved it. She was like: 'Oh, this is a great letter. You actually gave this to the president?' I said: 'Yeah, and I got in lots of trouble for it.'"

Hodges did not mind that his letter was leaked to the media in 1991. But it made him a marked man. He remained with the Bulls and, the following year, emulated Larry Bird by becoming the only other player in NBA history to win three successive three-point contests at the all-star weekend—showcasing his skill in sinking long-range shots.

Hodges won $20,000, and asked his fellow Bulls to join him in each pooling a similar amount from their vast earnings to help local communities. His teammates avoided the invitation, saying they would need to clear it with their agents. Hodges was disappointed, because "I envisioned the Chicago Bulls making history in the most meaningful way. We also had a basketball player [Jordan] whose popularity exceeded that of the pope. If the Bulls spoke in a collective voice during the golden age of professional basketball, the world would listen."

In his absorbing book, Hodges stresses how he tried repeatedly to persuade Jordan to "break with Nike and go into the sneaker business for himself, with the aim of creating jobs in the black communities." Jordan argued he was not in a position to take control while he was tainted by, allegedly, saying: "Republicans buy sneakers, too."

The veracity of that quote might be hazy, but Jordan, unlike Hodges, clearly avoided political engagement. Kareem Abdul-Jabbar, such a force in the NBA in the 1970s and '80s, said Jordan chose "commerce over conscience."

On 29 April 1992, with the Bulls cruising through the play-offs, the Los Angeles riots broke out after the four LAPD officers were cleared of all charges resulting from their savage assault on King. That same day, Jordan scored 56 points against the Miami Heat. Asked to comment on the King verdict, Jordan said: "I need to know more about it."

Rioting spread across LA for six days and Hodges followed the televised news—noticing how often, amid play-off fever, a "Be Like Mike" commercial in homage to Jordan was repeated. After game two of the 1992 championship final against Portland, Hodges was asked about the NBA's lack of black owners. He spoke out against racism in the NBA, and across America, and criticised Jordan for failing to address the judicial injustice towards King.

The *New York Times* ran the story; and Hodges' career was effectively over. Twenty-five days after Chicago became champions again, Hodges was told he would not be offered a new deal. He had just turned 32—but Hodges had been part of successive title-winning campaigns and remained king of the three-pointers.

Hodges' knowledge of the game and enduring shooting skills could not compensate for his political conviction. His belief that Jordan and his agent Dave Falk were, in tandem with others, "going to run me out of the league" came true. Not one NBA team would offer a contract to a free agent of huge experience.

His precarious situation deteriorated when his own agent, Bob Woolf, said he could no longer represent him. Hodges could not even find a new agent. "No one would return my calls," he remembers. While he waited forlornly for an offer from the NBA, which never came, Hodges played in Italy.

Unlike when Ali, John Carlos and Tommie Smith made powerful gestures of political defiance in the civil rights-enflamed 1960s, Hodges was an outcast. "It was a different climate. A brother facing oppression in the 1960s felt it the same, whether he was a bus driver or Ali. Look what the brothers did in Mexico City [when Carlos and Smith raised their fists in black power salutes during the playing of the Star Spangled Banner on the Olympic podium in 1968]. They faced unemployment and disenfranchisement.

"I had that too but, in my era, not many people stood up. The climate was very conservative—and it got worse because athletes were afraid to speak because of the ramifications I faced."

In his foreword to Hodges' book, the sportswriter Dave Zirin recalls that, when he started covering the NBA in 2003, he asked players why they did not speak out politically. The stock answer, fed to the players by their agents, was stark: "You don't want to be like Craig Hodges."

That troubling quote is echoed by Kaepernick's failure to win a new contract now he is no longer a quarterback for the San Francisco 49ers. Hodges is sympathetic. "The cruel part about it, man, is he's speaking on behalf of people who can't speak for themselves. Now he's spoken, it seems his platform has been removed. It's like [the NFL] are saying: 'We're going to take him away because we don't want his views to catch fire. We don't want him in a locker room spreading this truth.

"I applaud Colin. I'm trying to reach out to the brother so I can let him know personally: 'I respect you. If there's anything I can do please don't hesitate to call me. I've got your back.' I know he loves to play the game. So not getting a contract is hurtful to his essence. The fact he's not even getting offers right now is depressing for me, for him. I know these feelings."

But Hodges believes the outpouring of support for Kaepernick, especially on social media, "has to be heartening for him. He must know that, 'Hey man, I'm doing the right thing.'"

Hodges, in contrast, received no support. "None at all. Today, on social media, people can vibe with you even if they can't do anything about your opportunity to play. So I feel good he knows people support him. Now, if the NFL doesn't stump up and he doesn't get an opportunity, fans who are supportive of Colin should show their displeasure and stage a boycott. Don't buy jerseys or don't go to the game to show appreciation for his stance."

The way in which social media has publicised campaigns such as Black Lives Matter has meant sportsmen can no longer plead ignorance as Jordan and Scottie Pippen once did. When Hodges tried to get his teammates to read more about black history, Pippen supposedly said: "What do I need education for? I make six figures."

Hodges harbors no animosity towards Pippen or even Jordan. "Michael didn't speak out largely because he didn't know what to say—not because he was a bad person."

It should also be pointed out that Jordan chose to snub President Bush's invitation when the Bulls visited him in 1991. "I'm not going to the White House," Hodges remembers Jordan saying. "F--k Bush. I didn't vote for him."

How does he regard Jordan, 25 years on? "He's a savvy businessman. I applaud him for that, I don't hate on that. But he's gained knowledge through life experience and he has been getting into decent projects. I'm sure he is more conscious now."

Phil Jackson was the only man in the Chicago locker room to share Hodges' unhappiness at America's bombing of Iraq in 1991. "We get stuck in one idea of patriotism," Hodges says, "and if I don't march to the beat of that soundbite I'm unpatriotic. Me and Phil were different. When the Gulf War broke out in 1991, on Dr. King Day, actually, everybody said: 'We need to bomb the shit out of them.' Phil let them finish and he said: 'If we do that, then remember that's going to leave an orphan who will feel the pain as he grows up with the idea of revenge. Don't be too quick to cheer—because retaliation is in his hands now.'"

Jackson ended Hodges' 13-year isolation from the NBA when he offered him a coaching role at the LA Lakers. Hodges won two more championships with Jackson and the Lakers. The old wounds have healed but surely he despairs when, apart from the continuing loss of young black lives, Trump is in the White House?

"You would love to think we've come a long way, and that's saddening to me at times. The imagery portrays that black people have come a long way. We had a black president so we now can't talk about race any more? But we're still the least represented people in this nation."

Hodges dismisses Barack Obama's presidency. "He did some good things, I'm sure," Hodges snorts, "but I don't know what they are. Maybe he tried to get healthcare for everybody, but they're still running it the way they want."

Yet replacing Obama with Trump must dishearten Hodges? "No. It's not disheartening because there are natural cycles of life. We have been so mis-educated we don't understand there is a supreme answer. You know that old song—"Age of Aquarius"? It's about the dawning of a new age. It's coming, even if Trump says we're going to make America great again. For me, as a black man, when was America great? What's so great about the founding fathers, the civil war, the killing of Martin Luther King, the killing of Malcolm X? The blackballing of athletes during that period? What period are you talking about when America was great?

"But we are going to win, eventually, because poor people will rise, the disenfranchised will be franchised, and that franchisement ain't coming by no political act. It's coming from time and energy where people are getting tired of the bulls--t. It will happen naturally. Social media shows us many people have the same feeling as Colin Kaepernick. They're just not as visible. But there's a grassroots thing going on. It's a feeling in America right now, especially among young people, that something has to be done. Everyday life matters. Not just Black Lives Matter. We all matter."

Far from stressing over Trump, or lamenting the millions he lost when shut out of the NBA, Hodges sounds cheerful. "My son Jamaal loves to tell me: 'You're the Forrest Gump of basketball because of all the people you met. You've crossed paths with people that have been so illuminating.' He's right. Take this conversation between you and me."

Hodges and I have swapped notes about him growing up in Chicago while I was a small boy living under apartheid in South Africa—where Arthur Ashe was banned from playing tennis because he was black. "You can't tell me that there ain't some creator in all of this. That's why I say there are cycles of time and natural rhythms of law which change things and bring us together. The fact you and I are having this conversation is cool. We have a young brother that was in South Africa when they wouldn't allow Arthur Ashe, and a brother that was in Chicago watching Arthur Ashe trying to go to South Africa. Now you and me are talking.

"All the boundaries and divisions between us are manmade. And the human family is starting to cast that [expletive] off. It was a South African, Nelson Mandela, who gave me hope at my lowest point, when I was out of the NBA. He had been freed a few months earlier [after 27 years in prison] and he came to Chicago. There was a dinner in his honor and Mandela asked to sit next to me. I grew up in the projects, man. So that's a power bigger than me. I was in awe. I kept asking him: 'What was it like to be away from your people for so long?' He was amazing. Truth gave him power. He didn't need to be anyone other than himself. That's freedom."

Hodges has also found freedom. He will keep teaching basketball and speaking out—amid his belief that, finally, justice will prevail despite the political system and bleak shootings. "We'll win all our battles in the end. Until then I'm just doing what I can to keep children out of harm's way as much as possible. It's the right way."

7

Ex-Quarterback Jack Kemp Guided Ronald Reagan's Economic Policy

Michael Carlson

Michael Carlson is an American freelance broadcaster, journalist, writer, television pundit, and producer who lives in England. He covers the National Football League for the United Kingdom. As a television broadcaster, he is known for his witty commentary.

Jack Kemp was an undersized quarterback for the NFL's Buffalo Bills, but as a politician and senator from New York he had an oversized effect on economic policy. A fiscal conservative who was more liberal on social issues, Kemp championed "supply-side economics," which George H. W. Bush once labeled "voodoo economics" and others called "trickle down" economics. Kemp was an influence on a number of quarterbacks and other athletes who later became conservative politicians. Despite their mutual antagonism during the Republican primary lead-up to the 1996 presidential election, he was Bob Dole's choice for vice-president in Dole's failed campaign against Bill Clinton.

They were an unlikely pair to have changed the course of economic history, an ex-actor and a former professional gridiron star, but had not Jack Kemp, who has died aged 73, convinced Ronald Reagan to adopt "supply side" economics, the past 30 years would look very different. Both men owed

"US Politician Who Championed 'Supply Side' Economics," by Michael Carlson, Guardian News and Media Limited, May 4, 2009. Reprinted by permission.

their political careers to popularity gained as entertainers, but Kemp's career stalled on the wider stage after his failed run at the 1988 Republican presidential nomination, and his 1996 defeat as Bob Dole's vice-presidential running mate.

Labelled a "bleeding-heart" conservative because of his commitment to racial equality and many issues of social justice, Kemp was also a true believer, not least in what [George H. W. Bush] famously called "voodoo economics." Republicans happily embraced the tax cuts enacted by the Kemp-Roth legislation he sponsored along with Senator William Roth in 1981, but just as happily ignored the party's traditional commitment to balanced budgets; Reagan's budget deficit was unmatched in peacetime, until the second President Bush. Indeed, the long-term effect of freeing so much capital for the wealthy was to accelerate the development of new forms of investment, which have only recently come toppling down.

In America it is not unusual for sportsmen to pursue careers in politics; but after Kemp, a spate of former footballers arrived in Congress, all of them conservative and most of them, like Kemp, former quarterbacks. The quarterback is the leader and public face of his team, one of the few players in the spotlight of what is, for most of his teammates, an anonymous group effort. Kemp's leadership was evident in Congress; it also contributed to his failure to achieve higher office. The Republican strategist Edward Rollins told the *Los Angeles Times* that Kemp refused to bend his specific philosophical points in order to widen his appeal. "Quarterbacks think they can always make the big play and resent being controlled by anyone," he explained.

Kemp was born in Los Angeles, where his father ran a trucking company and his mother was a social worker. Working at the family firm provided the foundation for his affinity with minorities, something his sports career reinforced. A football and athletics star at the then largely Jewish Fairfax High, Kemp was too small to interest football powers such as Southern California or UCLA, and wound up starring at little Occidental College, where he met his wife, Joanne Main. Chosen late in the National Football League (NFL) college draft, he was released by five NFL teams, and one in Canada, before signing on in 1960 with the upstart American Football League's Los Angeles Chargers, then two years later with the Buffalo Bills. When the AFL merged with the NFL in 1970, Kemp had played in all 10 AFL seasons; making him arguably the league's most successful quarterback. He had also been instrumental in founding the AFL players' union.

He had taken graduate courses, but was largely an autodidact in political philosophy, starting with Ayn Rand and Margaret Thatcher's guru Friedrich von Hayek while, as his teammate Elbert Dubenion joked, "we were reading the Katzenammer kids." He campaigned for Barry Goldwater and Richard Nixon, and on gubernatorial efforts by Reagan in California and Nelson Rockefeller in New York, and Republicans were rewarded when his popularity in Buffalo won him a marginal seat in Congress in 1970; his district would be consistently re-zoned to become more solidly Republican during his 18 years in the House. "Pro football gave me a good perspective," he said. "When I entered the political arena, I had already been booed, cheered, cut, sold, traded, and hung in effigy."

In 1976 he was converted to Arthur Laffer's theories of "supply side" economics, and though he failed in three attempts to pass a bill offering across-the-board tax cuts, he succeeded, in 1979, in persuading Reagan's staff to make it a centrepiece of their campaign; after the 1980 election, he sponsored the tax-cutting Kemp-Roth legislation.

Kemp saw himself as the natural conservative successor to Reagan, but as [George H. W. Bush] and Dole battled in the early 1988 primaries, the evangelist Pat Robertson siphoned off too much of Kemp's support, and he withdrew. Bush might have chosen Kemp as his vice-president, but settled on the less-established Dan Quayle. After winning the election, Bush offered Kemp the one cabinet position, short of Treasury, he could not refuse, secretary of housing and urban development, where his socially liberal instincts generally ran foul of Republican policy. Although he and Dole displayed their mutual dislike during the 1980s—with Dole asking if Kemp claimed a "hairspray allowance" while Kemp accused Dole of having only two books, and not having coloured in one of them— in 1996 he balanced Dole's ticket by being conservative, Eastern, and younger. But Kemp's appeal to minority voters, after he had publicly opposed California's legislation aimed at illegal immigrants, was muted in the face of Bill Clinton's popularity.

He ran his own lobbying firm, Kemp Partners, and founded the Foundation for the Defense of Democracies, to counter the "terrorist threat" after 9/11. He had a syndicated newspaper column, and co-chaired the Russian Task Force for the Council of Foreign Relations.

He is survived by his wife, two daughters and two sons, both of whom were professional football quarterbacks.

8

Tim Tebow Has Exploited His Status as a Professional Athlete to Build a Conservative Christian Brand

Matt Hawzen

Matt Hawzen is Assistant Professor of Sports Administration at Fairleigh Dickinson University. His interests include media representations of sport celebrities, conservative politics in sport and physical culture, and labor relations in the sports industry.

Tim Tebow, the former Heisman Trophy winner and NFL quarterback with the Denver Broncos, has reinvented himself as a baseball player in the New York Mets farm system. Despite Tebow's limited success on the gridiron and the baseball diamond, his devout Christianity has served him well. Tebow's astounding popularity owes to the Christian fundamentalist media and its shrewd marketing. Tebow is a hero for white Christian America, and, as such, has thrived in the age of President Donald Trump, another hero of Christian fundamentalists. Hawzen argues that Tebow's privileged background has given him the opportunity, despite his limited abilities, to play professional sports, from which platform he builds a conservative Christian brand.

Five years since Tim Tebow and "Tebow Mania" flooded mainstream media, electoral politics, and religious discourse, the genuflecting born-again Christian is relevant in American sport culture once again. Though Tebow no longer throws

"Tim Tebow's Baseball Rebirth in Trump's America," by Matt Hawzen, March 21, 2017. Reprinted by permission.

fluttering passes in the NFL, the barrel-chested southpaw now crowds the plate at First Data Field in Port St. Lucie, Florida for the New York Mets in spring training. On September 5, 2016, the Mets signed Tebow to a minor league contract that included a $100,000 signing bonus.

The Denver Broncos drafted Tebow 25th overall in the 2010 NFL draft and signed him to an $11.25 million contract despite signs that Tebow was not an NFL caliber quarterback. The scouting report leading up to the NFL draft provided clear suggestions that Tebow may struggle. Even when he performed relatively well, pundits maintained, "he just can't play," with some suggesting he was worse than notoriously bad NFL quarterbacks Ryan Leaf and Jamarcus Russell. Tebow is now a 29 year-old "prospect" who signed with the Mets despite not having played organized baseball since high school. Wandering in left field and stiff at the plate, in his 2016 fall league debut Tebow hit under .200 and struck out in 20 of 62 at-bats. Longtime baseball analyst Keith Law described him as a "farce" and "imposter pretending to have talent."

Many have suggested that the Mets are "shamefully" employing Tebow's athletic talent, or lack thereof, in so far as he continues to bring reliable merchandise sales and valuable branding to the club. After proving incapable at quarterback, Tebow bounced around the NFL as a backup with three different teams from 2012 to 2015, received very little playing time, yet still managed to lead the league in jersey sales. Tebow's Mets jersey, selling for up to $119.00, is already a league leader.

Tebow's particular branding is part of a broader history of Christian fundamentalist media and marketing that Steinberg and Kincheloe (2008) call Christotainment. Christotainment refers to the commercialization of Christianity, particularly in television and radio entertainment, that spreads conservative Christian ideas and American recovery narratives (e.g., "Making America Great Again"), and serves white supremacy. Since the 1960s, Christotainment has been dedicated to remaking the image

of Jesus into a hero for white men and boys. This new symbol of
Jesus represents conservative ideals, American nationalism, and
the masculine strength to "recover" what, it is perceived, has been
"lost" in America such as patriarchy, "nuclear" family values, and
white dominance in the economy and electoral politics. Tebow's
public image is not intolerant or explicitly in service of white
identities in these ways. Rather, Tebow is a "softer" face, and
sporting spectacle, of this recovery heroism.

Branding is meant to bolster private entities' appeal to
consumers and generate income. Tebow's brand appears as a
non-brand, if you will, because it is of God's image, good will,
and giving back to communities. This brand and public image
is about "giving" rather than "receiving" from consumers. The
meanings of Tebow's brand are exemplified in his non-profit Tim
Tebow Foundation, a globalized community outreach charity
with a mission "to bring Faith, Hope and Love to those needing
a brighter day in their darkest hour of need." Making money off
this kind of brand might seem antithetical, if not unethical, but
it is crucial for Tebow to 1) become a professional football and
baseball "prospect" who gets offered lucrative contracts and multi-
million dollar endorsements; 2) sell Tebow-commodities, such
as two autobiographies and Tim Tebow Foundation jewelry; 3)
use sport and the media to evangelize; and, 4) as my research
with Josh Newman demonstrates, fit the "pro-life" Super Bowl
commercial message in which he was featured, and promote
conservative Christian recovery, persecution, and white-male
victimhood narratives.

Tebow's brand has been built upon a lifetime of opportunity
and privilege in social life and in sport. If anyone was meant
to succeed in sport, it was Tebow. This is not a rags-to-riches
story by any means. According to his autobiography, Tebow was
homeschooled by his mother, which afforded him the leisure time
to develop his large physical frame. He routinely worked out and
consumed protein shakes plus other supplements that contributed
to his physical strength and athleticism. His born-again parents

are also land-owners whose finances and Christian networks afforded Tebow the opportunity to experience foreign cultures where he became privy to public relations practices. Ultimately, in order to play quarterback as a homeschooled athlete, Tebow lived in a spare apartment owned by his family in another county, allowing him to play football at a Florida public school. Tebow eventually parlayed this upbringing into a full-ride scholarship to the football powerhouse University of Florida. He now compounds this privilege, rife with opportunity, into an over-extended, deeply commercialized career that combines a supposedly not-financially-motivated innocence with dogmatic, conservative Christian commentary about society.

Yet when he was released by the New England Patriots in 2015, Tebow's commercial and ideological opportunism became apparent. He turned this new chapter into more media exposure, another lucrative autobiography, a six-figure contract, and a well-worn American Dream trope. Consider his message in a recent interview with ESPN about people who doubt his latest baseball pursuits: "It is unfortunate in society," Tebow explained, that people just "live with the status quo … live by all these rules, and … just accept [the] average nine-to-five rather than striving for something" more.

In this statement on American society, Tim Tebow, a millionaire, is ironically recasting himself as a symbol of hardship and perseverance, as a surrogate for new conservative responses to structural inequality, diversity, and lack of opportunity. Which is to say, "if Tebow can do it, anyone can." Tebow's version of the American Dream works for privileged people like himself in Trump's America, and against many underprivileged populations including people of color, members of the working class, and, in this case, non-Christians, as well as the actual baseball prospects who have been stripped of opportunity because of how Tebow's brand provides value for team owners.

In short, Tebow's privileged background gives him ample access to professional sport where he builds a conservative Christian brand. This brand possesses economic value for professional sport franchises, presents Tebow with more (undeserved) opportunity, and has cultural value in, and for, contemporary conservatism in American society.

9

Billie Jean King Has Made a Profound Impact on Sports and on Society

Jo Ward

Jo Ward is a PhD candidate in psychology. She is a former professional tennis player, a coach, and a coach educator.

Tennis champion Billie Jean King is as much a legend for her social activism as she is for her accomplishments on the court. Her famous "Battle of the Sexes" tennis match against Bobby Riggs was ostensibly a sporting event, but it was really about social change, about the ability of women to take their rightful place side-by-side with men in sports and society. Women athletes like Serena Williams have followed in King's footsteps to fight for equality, but there is still a long way to go. Women athletes continue to struggle for equal pay and respect.

In 1973, an unusual tennis match attracted an enormous amount of attention. Around 90m people around the world watched the women's champion Billie Jean King take on Bobby Riggs, who had been men's world number one in the 1940s. Dubbed the Battle of the Sexes, it was arranged after Riggs repeatedly poured scorn on women's tennis.

Before the match, the players exchanged gifts. Bobby gave Billie a giant Sugar Daddy lollipop. She returned the gesture by presenting him with a pig.

"Battle of the Sexes: Four Decades After Billie Jean King's Triumph, Women Still Fight for Equal Billing in Sports," by Jo Ward, The Conversation, November 17, 2017. https:// theconversation.com/battle-of-the-sexes-four-decades-after-billie-jean-kings-triumph-women-still-fight-for-equal-billing-in-sports-87539. Licensed under CC-BY 4.0.

The symbolism wasn't meant to be subtle. This was a match between feminism and chauvinism—and much more was at stake than the US$100,000 prize money, especially for King. She had left the professional tour, due to the earning disparity (men received 12 times as much as women in some events) and was leading the newly formed Women's Tennis Association (WTA).

King, and feminism, triumphed in the match—she won 6-4, 6-3, 6-3—which has now been made into a film starring Emma Stone and Steve Carell. But have things really moved on since 1973?

On the surface things look pretty good. For a decade, women and men have received equal pay at all four tennis grand slams. Wimbledon was the last bastion of inequality in prize money, but eventually bowed to pressure from a host of female players, led by Venus Williams, in 2007.

Tennis is the only sport to boast a female in the Forbes Highest Paid Athletes list of 2017 (Serena Williams at #51), and draws large viewing figures in which the women at times eclipse the men. The financial status of female tennis players has certainly evolved.

But have attitudes changed enough since Riggs declared that women belonged "in the bedroom and kitchen"? The recent scandals in Hollywood and Westminster might suggest not. Even within tennis there is still an undercurrent of chauvinism that has profound implications on female performance and participation.

Locker Room Talk

Just last year Raymond Moore, boss of the Indian Wells Tournament, suggested that the WTA Tour was "very lucky" because it "rides on the coat-tails of the men." He suggested that women players should "go down every night on [their] knees and thank God that Roger Federer and Rafa Nadal were born." He later apologised and retracted his comments after a spate of negative responses, including from King.

> *Billie Jean King*
> *@BillieJeanKing*
> *Disappointed in #RaymondMoore comments. He is wrong on so many levels. Every player, especially the top players, contribute to our success*
>   *5:46 PM - Mar 20, 2016*

Then John McEnroe claimed that if Serena Williams played the men's circuit, "she'd be, like, 700 in the world." His comments led to a predictable outpouring of chauvinism on social media.

On a more positive note, Andy Murray continues to fight casual sexism with his unique blend of boredom and disdain. He corrected a journalist who stated that Sam Querrey was "the first US player to reach a major semi-final since 2009." "Male player," Murray reminded him, with his head almost in hands. And when congratulated by a TV host who wrongly suggested Murray was the first player to win two Olympic golds, he shot back with a smile: "I think Venus and Serena have won about four each."

But, notwithstanding Murray's support, there is a serious problem with the negative stereotypes that still pervade sport. This is a phenomenon known as "stereotype threat." The psychological effect of stereotypes and their impact on performance has been studied across myriad domains—including the effect on women in sport.

So while there are obvious and observable differences between men and women, biology alone might not be the whole picture. Women and men are operating in entirely different psychological climates.

Female athletes and sports are invisible in the media, receiving only a 7% share of coverage. Every time you turn on the TV or read a sports article, the coverage reinforces the stereotype that sport is for men.

Females are also vastly outnumbered in participation. In the UK there are 2m fewer women than men regularly playing sport, further entrenching the view that sport is a man's world. If being invisible and outnumbered weren't problematic enough, women and girls also contend with negative stereotypes that span both ends of an equally pernicious continuum from not being athletic enough to not being feminine or pretty enough.

With all this distraction it's a wonder that women can perform at all athletically. And it's no surprise that, even when sport can attract girls, those numbers plummet as girls drop out during puberty—just 12% of girls aged 14 meet the official guidelines for physical activity.

Love All

Sport needs a culture change. Even with the heavy psychological burden of negative stereotypes, there are amazing examples of female athleticism, which don't get the attention they deserve. There are women who can sprint 100m to within a second of Usain Bolt. That's a 10% difference, I know, but I defy anyone to claim it's not athletic.

Sabine Lisicki rocketed a 131mph serve in 2014, faster than anything Roger Federer has hit in years. Women achieve incredible feats all the time—but for as long as comparisons are drawn with men they will continue to be ignored and little girls will continue to be denied their role models.

To spin it a different way, no one would dare suggest that distance runner Mo Farah is less of an athlete than Bolt because he can't run as fast. Or that boxer Manny Pacquiao is less sporty than Anthony Joshua because he doesn't hit as hard. So why do so many men insist on comparing male and female athletes in such a pointless way?

It's time we started really celebrating women for the work they put in and the performances they produce. Until more amazing women are visible, it will continue to be only a minority of women who survive and thrive in sport.

Until we get equal opportunity, exposure and respect, to match the hard-won equal prize money, there is much work to do. There have been gains, but attitudes still haven't changed enough to make sport a welcome place for women. Forty-four years after King's victory, the battle continues.

Colin Kaepernick's Right to Kneel Has Already Been Upheld in the Supreme Court

Larry Kummer

Larry Kummer is editor of the Fabius Maximus *website. He formerly worked in the financial industry as a senior portfolio manager and Vice President of Investments. His articles are widely reposted, appearing in Roubini's Economonitor, Investing.com, OilPrice.com, Wolf Street, and Seeking Alpha, among other sites.*

When NFL quarterback Colin Kaepernick began to kneel during the National Anthem before games, perhaps no one was quite prepared for the controversy that would erupt. Kaepernick knelt to protest the oppression of people of color by American authorities, particularly the police. The backlash against Kaepernick was immediate and sustained. But many see Kaepernick's position as a constitutional right. In 1943, the US Supreme Court heard arguments concerning a West Virginia law that forced students and teachers to salute the flag. In a majority opinion, Justice Robert H. Jackson wrote that West Virginia's law was unconstitutional and violated the First and Fourteenth Amendments. Censuring Kaepernick is a similar violation of the quarterback's right to freedom of speech.

"Looking Beyond the Politics of the Kneeling NFL Players," by Larry Kummer, Fabius Maximus, 09/26/2017. https://fabiusmaximus.com/2017/09/26/beyond-politics-of-the-kneeling-nfl-players/. Licensed under CC BY 4.0 International.

The controversy over the NFL players kneeling during performance of the "Star Spangled Banner." There are multiple threads to this kerfuffle.

> *I am not going to stand up to show pride in a flag for a country that oppresses black people and people of color. To me, this is bigger than football and it would be selfish on my part to look the other way. There are bodies in the street and people getting paid leave and getting away with murder.*
>
> *—San Francisco 49ers quarterback Colin Kaepernick to NFL Media on 26 August 2016. He opted out of his 49[ers] contract in March 2017. He remains unemployed by any NFL team.*

> *The national anthem is and always will be a special part of the pre-game ceremony. It is an opportunity to honor our country and reflect on the great liberties we are afforded as its citizens. In respecting such American principles as freedom of religion and freedom of expression, we recognize the right of an individual to choose and participate, or not, in our celebration of the national anthem."*
>
> *—Statement by the management of the San Francisco 49[ers].*

First, there is the bizarre involvement of Trump, our clown president. He has gotten involved in this for the same reason President Carter scheduled the White House tennis courts they are lost in the job and focus on trivia that they understand. Except that Trump's Twitter belligerence is worse than Carter's harmless peccadillo.

Second, there is the conflict of values between NFL players (70% African-American, with incomes starting at $465,000 and soaring into the millions) and their largely white blue-collar fans (15% African-American, 26% earning $40k or less, 35% earning over $75k). Fans pay for expensive seats in stadiums built largely with their taxes—to watch political demonstrations from people with 10x their income. If this continues, the fans reaction could be big—and bad for the business of football.

Third, there is patriotism. Is this a fit subject for the president to interject himself (and so implicitly the government) into? Second, is it a good idea to make patriotic rituals—such as standing for the national anthem—be compulsory? The words of one of the Supreme Court's landmark decisions illuminates both questions.

On June 14, 2018, people in the United States—many, and indeed most, people, I hope—will mark and celebrate the 75th anniversary of the Supreme Court's decision in *West Virginia State Board of Education v. Barnette*. In that landmark decision, the Court struck down as unconstitutional the State's requirement that all public school teachers and students participate in a salute to the American flag and a recitation of the Pledge of Allegiance.

The case was brought on behalf of students who were Jehovah's Witnesses. In deference to their belief that the Bible forbade them to bow down to graven images, they refused to salute the flag. For that refusal, they were expelled from school. Expulsion made the children unlawfully absent, subjecting them to delinquency proceedings and their parents to criminal prosecution.

The *Barnette* decision was announced in Justice Robert H. Jackson's opinion for Court. He explained that the flag salute requirement violated the children's constitutional rights, which exist to strengthen "individual freedom of mind in preference to officially disciplined uniformity …"

Although all of Justice Jackson's *Barnette* opinion bears rereading, some particularly wise words to consider are his closing paragraphs:

> *The case is made difficult not because the principles of its decision are obscure, but because the flag involved is our own. Nevertheless, we apply the limitations of the Constitution with no fear that freedom to be intellectually and spiritually diverse or even contrary will disintegrate the social organization. To believe that patriotism will not flourish if patriotic ceremonies are voluntary and spontaneous, instead of a compulsory routine, is*

*to make an unflattering estimate of the appeal of our institutions
to free minds.*

*We can have intellectual individualism and the rich cultural
diversities that we owe to exceptional minds only at the price of
occasional eccentricity and abnormal attitudes. When they are
so harmless to others or to the State as those we deal with here,
the price is not too great. But freedom to differ is not limited to
things that do not matter much. That would be a mere shadow
of freedom. The test of its substance is the right to differ as to
things that touch the heart of the existing order.*

*If there is any fixed star in our constitutional constellation,
it is that no official, high or petty, can prescribe what shall be
orthodox in politics, nationalism, religion, or other matters
of opinion, or force citizens to confess by word or act their
faith therein. If there are any circumstances which permit an
exception, they do not now occur to us.*

*We think the action of the local authorities in compelling the
flag salute and pledge transcends constitutional limitations on
their power, and invades the sphere of intellect and spirit which
it is the purpose of the First Amendment to our Constitution to
reserve from all official control.*

In the views of many, *Barnette* is a high point in US Supreme
Court history and constitutional law and one of Justice Jackson's
very finest judicial opinions. His words in *Barnette* continue to
ring, loudly and true, to people who think them through.

One example came from the Supreme Court itself in June
2013, *Barnette*'s 70th anniversary year and month. In *Agency for
International Development v. Alliance for Open Society International,
Inc.*, the Court struck down as unconstitutional the part of an
international program to combat HIV/AIDS that required grant
recipients to "pledge allegiance to the Government's policy of
eradicating prostitution."

With regard to that government effort to compel a pledge,
Chief Justice Roberts wrote for the Supreme Court that "we
cannot improve upon what Justice Jackson wrote for the Court
70 years ago: 'If there is any fixed star in our constitutional

constellation, it is that no official, high or petty, can prescribe what shall be orthodox in politics, nationalism, religion, or other matters of opinion, or force citizens to confess by word or act their faith therein.'"

11

Football Legend Jim Brown Has Lost His Way as an Activist

Ricardo Hazell

Ricardo A. Hazell has served as senior contributor with The Shadow League *website since 2013, where he covers black cultural angles that intersect with the mainstream news. His work has appeared in the* Washington Post, *the* Chicago Tribune, *the* South China Sea Morning Post, *the Root, and many other publications.*

In the following viewpoint, Ricardo Hazell examines the changing politics of former NFL running back Jim Brown. Brown is often regarded as arguably the greatest NFL player ever. He was also a committed activist, whose opinions were sought out alongside those of superstars Kareem Abdul-Jabbar, Bill Russell, and Muhammad Ali. But Brown, once a paragon of black manhood, has fallen in line behind President Donald Trump, whose policies have not favored black Americans. Perhaps Brown was never quite the man his public image led us to believe, says Hazell. Brown's voice is no longer relevant in discussions of social issues.

J im Brown was at one time the consensus best football player to ever play in the National Football League but he's no longer that guy. Once upon a time, he was considered by some to be the prototype of black masculinity. I can still recall movies like *The Dirty Dozen, Condor* and *Black Gunn*, as well as those pop posters

"The Aging of Jim Brown from Social Activist to Republican Minion," by Ricardo Hazell, The Shadow League, August 28, 2017. Reprinted by permission.

featuring Brown with his shirt posing alongside a model. He's not that guy anymore either. I also recall the Jim Brown that was so fed up with the manner in which the late Art Modell demanded he leave the movie set of *The Dirty Dozen* and report to training camp that he immediately retired.

By now most of us know that Jim Brown threw his hat in with Donald J. Trump and has even said that he has fallen in love with the controversial president who has shown a disdain for just about every demographic you can think of. The armor of this once shining knight of black manhood has rusted with age, but it may not have been as sturdy as we believed it to be in the first place.

Recently, the Cleveland Browns legend gave his thoughts on Colin Kaepernick after the entire Cleveland Browns team stood for the national anthem, after previously being fragmented in their approach. There are also reports that the team's decision to all stand for the anthem may have been influenced by Brown, who visited the locker room prior to kickoff. Brown said the NFL free agent needs to choose between being a football player and being an activist; as nonsensical a thing as I've heard all week. He also said that he must respect the flag and respect the national anthem.

The anti-Kaepernick contingent got a kick out of that. Just four years ago, Jim Brown admonished Kobe Bryant for not being more activist-minded and even lamented that modern athletes lacked Ali's resolve in 2012. What happened?

Brown was said to be a real man's man, someone who lived by his own code and didn't take kindly to being told what to do. When doing research on Brown, we see him as a former football great, a former actor and a civil rights activist. Also, there are plenty of photos floating around with Brown alongside other sports greats like Kareem Abdul-Jabbar, Bill Russell, former NFL players John Wooten, Walter Beach, Willie Davis and Bobby Mitchell, then Cleveland Mayor Carl Stokes, and of course Ali. The photo was taken after an intense two-hour exchange in which Brown and company bombarded Ali with questions to test the sincerity of reasoning as to why he did not wish to accept being drafted into the United States Army during the Vietnam War. The meeting, which took place in 1967, was the beginning of a long friendship between Brown and Ali.

The two men would go onto their respective destinies from that day forth. Ali would become the greatest heavyweight that ever lived and, for a longtime, one of the most recognized people in the world. Jim Brown would continue his activism; which included being heavily involved in the Stop the Violence movement of the late 80s and early 90s, being involved in an L.A. gang truce that was moderately successful and educating inner city children to the powerful potential that lay within them.

Indeed, because we loved everything that Jim Brown appeared to stand for, his very lengthy history of domestic violence was not even an afterthought as we showered accolades upon him for his football career, acting career, his involvement within impoverished urban communities and how he seemed to maintain the appearance of strength and virility well into his seventies.

Back in 2012, I lamented the absence of contemporary activist athletes in a piece called "Sports Activism Is Dead, Long Live Sports Activism," which was published in EURweb. As anyone else would have done, I mentioned Brown in the same breath as Ali, Russell and Jabbar. These were his contemporaries in more ways than one.

Fast forward to 2017 and it seems as if Brown has lost touch with society a bit. His attacks on Kaepernick for kneeling aren't consistent with his reputation as a civil rights activist. Not to beat a fossilized horse, but is he talking about the flag under which the Tuskegee Experiments, Jim Crow and the War on Drugs were all purposefully visited upon Black people in America?

Brown would have us respect and stand for the national anthem that has lyrics that appear to celebrate slavery? Riiiiiight. To be clear, I wouldn't advocate purposefully disrespecting these things. In fact, I think Kaep's decision to protest in the manner he did is very respectful and uber-American, apple pie and all. Taking a knee, rather than sitting, was clearly an attempt at showing some deference despite his stance.

Kaep has stated on many occasions that he has no plans to continue his on field protest this season, so why does he need to choose between the NFL and activism, again? Why would anyone stop trying to help the oppressed? The cat is out of the bag now as players from all over the National Football League are joining the protest against police brutality and oppression, and I suspect most of them won't be swayed by some former great. Kaepernick was the catalyst but never set himself up to be any kind of leader. Heck, I've never once heard Colin refer to himself as an activist, either.

Kaepernick is someone who has seen suffering, witnessed the unavenged deaths of the innocent and the callous hearts of the powers that be. He followed his conscience and, though he's no longer in the position to protest even if he wanted to, Kaep will continue being the topic of conversation from opponents to his actions. Why? To make an example out of him for all to see, virtually lynching his football career while pointing fingers at its shattered shell, laughing and smiling at what could have been. Because, while you may not be able to kill a dream, you can certainly demoralize a dreamer who has no support. Therefore, Kaep needs his supporters to remain steadfast now more than ever. And Jim Brown needs to sit down somewhere. He's irrelevant.

12

Sports Stars Are Taking a Knee Against Donald Trump

Keith Rathbone

Keith Rathbone is a lecturer in Modern European History and Sports History at Macquarie University in Australia.

Visits by championship sports teams to the White House are common, and, on the surface, apolitical. But according to Keith Rathbone, the truth is that they have always been politicized. With Donald Trump having criticized activist athletes such as Colin Kaepernick, such visits—or lack thereof—have become increasingly political. The NBA champion Golden State Warriors, for example, declined Trump's invitation, which sparked a Twitter war between the president and athletes such as LeBron James. According to Rathbone, athletes have for too long been used by politicians, and it is a positive development that they are now speaking out for themselves.

US President Donald Trump is continuing his public attacks on prominent black athletes. Late last week, he urged National Football League (NFL) team owners to fire players who knelt in protest during the playing of the national anthem before the game. "Get that son of a b**** off the field," Trump told a partisan crowd in the conservative state of Alabama.

The next day, he disinvited National Basketball Association (NBA) champion Steph Curry from the White House.

> *Donald J. Trump*
> > *@realDonaldTrump*
>
> *Going to the White House is considered a great honor for a championship team. Stephen Curry is hesitating, therefore invitation is withdrawn!*
> > *8:45 AM - Sep 23, 2017*

Trump's remarks rankled black athletes in the NBA and NFL. His disinvitation of Curry, who is black, sounded a racial dog-whistle to those who believe African-Americans do not belong in the White House.

Trump's subsequent Twitter statements about the NFL suggest deeply troubling assumptions about the proper place of black athletes in public spaces.

> *Donald J. Trump*
> > *@realDonaldTrump*
> *The issue of kneeling has nothing to do with race. It is about respect for our Country, Flag and National Anthem. NFL must respect this!*
> > *7:39 AM - Sep 25, 2017*

The History of White House Visits

The invitation of athletes to the White House appears apolitical. Presidents have customarily extended invitations to everyone from Little League World Series to Super Bowl winners. However, tradition has also always been intertwined with America's racial politics.

Major League Baseball (MLB) World Series winners have regularly visited the White House since the 1920s, before black athletes broke the colour line (they were excluded from playing in the league at the time).

The first NBA team to visit the White House was the Boston Celtics in 1963, invited by then-president John F. Kennedy. The 1960s Celtics represented white America in the face of an increasingly African-American league.

White House visits seem innocuous, but they are political spectacles, with handshakes, photos and memorabilia exchanges. When athletes meet the president, they are used as vehicles to promote specific policies.

In the waning years of the Cold War, Ronald Reagan used these visits to symbolise American power, vigour and confidence through athletic achievement. In 1988, for example, Reagan tossed a tight spiral to visiting NFL wide receiver Ricky Sanders. Cameras caught this moment and transformed the president into a game-winning quarterback.

Not all athletes appreciate being used as a tool for policy. Increasingly, they have rejected invitations to the White House to express their discontent. The boycotts by whole teams like Curry's Golden State Warriors, however, is a new kind of demonstration made even more powerful by the fame of their top players.

A few days after the NBA finals concluded, Curry promised to avoid the White House. His teammates have been effusive in their support of his stance. Coach Steve Kerr said "he [Trump] was going to break up with us before we could break up with him."

The team also released a statement:

In lieu of a visit to the White House, we have decided that we'll constructively use our trip to the nation's capital in February to celebrate equality, diversity, and inclusion—the values that we embrace as an organisation.

Trump's comments have had the unintended effect of galvanising support of the whole league behind the Warriors. NBA players have taken to Twitter to openly mock him. The NBA's biggest star, LeBron James, tweeted:

LeBron James
  @KingJames
U bum @StephenCurry30 already said he ain't going! So therefore ain't no invite. Going to White House was a great honor until you showed up!
  11:17 AM - Sep 23, 2017

Alluding to the investigation of the Trump campaign's ties with Russia, Robin Lopez tweeted:

> *Robin Lopez*
>   *@rolopez42*
> *It's ok @warriors, in a few months @realDonaldTrump probably won't be able to visit the White House either*
>   *5:22 PM - Sep 23, 2017*

Teeming Player Protests

In the NFL, then-San Francisco 49ers quarterback Colin Kaepernick's decision to kneel during the national anthem was a protest originally directed against police violence, not Trump (who was not president at the time).

But Trump's words have now shifted the debate onto him, added legitimacy to the demonstrations, and perhaps roused a force powerful enough to battle his own celebrity brand. Trump has taken on the NFL before and lost.

The NFL players' union and the NFL commissioner—two sides usually at loggerheads—expressed joint anger over Trump's intervention in the league's affairs. NFL commissioner Roger Goodell lamented Trump's "lack of respect" for the league. And the head of the union, DeMaurice Smith, defiantly thundered that the NFL Players Association would:

> *… never back down when it comes to protecting the constitutional rights of our players as citizens.*

The national anthem protests, which initially divided the league and the public, have become ubiquitous. On Sunday afternoon, whole teams, including the Pittsburgh Steelers, remained in their locker rooms in a forceful rejection of Trump's remarks. The Ravens and the Jaguars, playing in London, knelt for the American national anthem but stood respectfully for "God Save the Queen."

The kneeling players have been joined by team owners, performers and cheerleaders. The protest even spread to the more conservative and white MLB, when the Oakland A's Bruce Maxwell became the first player to kneel during the national anthem.

Trump's ill-timed comments have given legitimacy to claims of his racial animus. Until he disavows them, we can expect to see more players signalling their disapproval of his presidency.

The growing protests are a healthy new development for American sports. For too long, athletes have been the tools of statesmen. Today, however, they have begun to realise their power to be activists and undermine the political plans of the US president.

13

English Athlete Activists Are Making Their Mark on Society

Jon Holmes

Jon Holmes is a digital media editor and journalist who writes, edits, and manages sports content for web, mobile, and other platforms. He often writes about LBGTQ issues.

English hockey star and gold medalist Helen Richardson-Walsh and others like her have been encouraged by athlete activist role models such as Serena Williams, and they are attempting to do more to effect social change in their own country. For them, it's a time of opportunity to do good in the world. Richardson-Walsh has championed LGBTQ causes and has stated that transgender people still face discrimination despite the progress that has been made by others in the LGBTQ community. Other athletes, such as former wheelchair racer Tanni Gray-Thompson and climber Molly Thompson-Smith have also sought to use their platforms to bring about societal change by promoting equality and inclusiveness.

It's the "gumption" of the younger generation that gives Helen Richardson-Walsh hope for the future.

The Olympic gold medallist wants more sports stars to show they care about social issues by speaking out. She's seeing encouraging signs; that those coming through are getting more savvy about social media and are recognising the power of their

"Athlete Activism Upsurge Encouraging Next Generation to Speak Up for Social Causes," by Jon Holmes, Sky Uk, January 1, 2019. Reprinted by permission.

platforms. There's an improved understanding that you can be a high achiever and an athlete activist, but that it takes initiative and self-confidence to succeed at both. Richardson-Walsh is ready to help harness that enthusiasm.

"When I was younger, I'm not even sure I'd have recognised it was necessary," she admits, when asked if she would have felt so comfortable in the past to address inclusion, gender equality, and mental health. These are three issues which the hockey champion—who won almost 300 caps for England and Great Britain—has brought to wider attention through discussing her own experiences, at events, in interviews, and on social. But even in her youth—"I was a grumpy teen, often moaning"—it was never the case that she didn't care enough, just that she lacked direction.

A pointed comment from a teacher sticks in her memory. "She looked at me once after I'd complained about something, and said simply, 'What are you going to do about it?' It's only in recent years that I've truly started to appreciate what she meant."

Her sense of purpose is shared by the women alongside her on a panel discussion about Olympians and Paralympians' perspectives on social causes, being held at the relaunch event of the thinkBeyond Talent agency. Like Richardson-Walsh, Baroness Tanni Grey-Thompson participated in multiple Games before refocusing her energies to bring about change; next to her, Jade Jones-Hall is pursuing her own targets in paratriathlon as well as wider goals in access to disability sport; and Molly Thompson-Smith, a Sky Scholar, is using her journey towards Tokyo 2020 to raise awareness of the lack of diversity in climbing and adventure sports.

Together they represent Generations X, Y and Z, with Richardson-Walsh and Grey-Thompson familiar to medal podiums and public speaking, and Jones-Hall and Thompson-Smith eager to gain more experience of both. The aim of thinkBeyond Talent is to assist talent in identifying causes close to their hearts, and to best position them so that their words are heard, and their hard work gets results. In a video message after the panel chat,

Michael Johnson presents a showcase for his Young Leaders programme, while boxer Carl Frampton appears in person to discuss his commitment to community cohesion in his native Northern Ireland.

It's a time of opportunity, particularly for those in the UK who are picking up on the raised volume of athlete activism in the US. As a Serena Williams tweet earlier in the week put it, "Listen up. This is the voice of the athlete." Even by itself, that call to action would be strong, given Serena's personality and history, but it's galvanised further by the presence of the Nike logo. "Until We All Win" is a brand slogan that strives for equality and which people can buy into—in every sense.

Richardson-Walsh describes herself as "a massive Serena fan"; they were in fact born only a few days apart, and while both struck gold at Rio 2016, Helen would be the first to emphasise that their personal narratives and the size of their respective global audiences are vastly different. Yet in relative terms and through their individual sense of identity, both have become accomplished storytellers.

Helen's triumph with Team GB at Rio 2016 had added significance as it was achieved alongside her wife Kate, providing a milestone for LGBT visibility in sport. Her parents were special needs teachers, and the spirit of their work continues with the Richardson-Walshes serving as ambassadors for Access Sport on the Flyerz Hockey programme for disability hockey. In addition, Helen has spoken of her own experiences with depression in a bid to eliminate the stigma that surrounds mental health.

A commitment to participation for all underpins her inclusion work; she cites Flyerz as an example. "I feel like I'm coming from a place of privilege in certain areas, and that would be one of them.

"Everyone should grow up, regardless of who they are, with the opportunity to play sport. That's why I feel so passionate about disability hockey. When you see those people out there on the pitch, connecting, enjoying it, it takes me back to why I used to play. Sometimes it's easy to forget why we play sport, and what it can give.

"You can get just as much satisfaction out of helping someone else play, and seeing them develop, as you do yourself."

She is encouraged by the albeit slow progress on the visibility of lesbian, gay and bisexual people in sport—"it is important, and every year, it gets slightly better"—but debates around the T in LGBT frustrate her. "I try to put myself in different people's shoes, and this is one area where I've been disappointed with LGB people. I don't think there is that support that there should be for the trans community.

"In society, there absolutely isn't either. Trans people are going through what gay people went through in the 70s and 80s, and it doesn't need to be the case.

"In sport, I think governing bodies and associations need to really start talking about this. Recognising that there are trans people that want to play their sports is first and foremost. But the more vocal we are as a collective, the better it will be.

"Even for hockey, they struggled to support outwardly myself and Kate in our relationship. There is that fear factor, of not wanting to say or do the wrong thing. Whether those NGBs [national governing bodies] look more to Stonewall or they talk more to trans people in sport, they need to really try to understand what's necessary for inclusion. And that's only the starting point."

Richardson-Walsh continues to seek out answers herself; she now has a Masters in organisational psychology, with her studies providing a deeper knowledge of workplace behaviour, while also allowing her to apply academic thinking to the elite sports culture in which she grew up. In union with Kate, she has an ongoing pledge to "smash stereotypes" and is interested in how clever marketing can kickstart the kind of conversations that release people from their pigeonholes.

In the last week, she has attempted to stay across reactions to the new Gillette advert, titled "We Believe," which takes a didactic approach to how "men behaving badly" affects society.

The campaign launch has followed on from the release of a much-discussed American Psychological Association report on the dangers posed by traditional masculinity. So did Gillette get the tone right? "If everyone's talking about the ad, then it's probably having the impact they wanted. When we start talking, that's when stuff changes.

"But I don't see it as being about 'masculinity.'" The ad shows various scenarios where men act inappropriately towards women. "Really, it's about how we pick up on what's wrong. It's saying we should treat people the right way."

Later, Richardson-Walsh cites another Procter & Gamble campaign—Always' #LikeAGirl—which first ran five years ago and used examples from sport, society, and the more limited emoji library of the times, to show how girls and young women received a stream of negative signals in their day-to-day lives. "We live in a constructed world," she explains, "that puts stereotypes—which are limiting and excluding—in our heads. That leads us to take shortcuts, and to put things into groups." During the panel chat, she asks the audience to be mindful of that and to leave a space between thought and action; room to manoeuvre around the stereotype.

Thompson-Smith is still at the beginning of her career as an athlete but is equally determined to inspire others. "I want to teach girls that it's cool to be strong, and to take on adventure sports," she says. The 21-year-old is already working with British climbing's governing body, the BMC, to make the sport more accessible to BAME people and women, producing content and video and tailoring introductory sessions so that new starters come back for more. "I've heard girls say, 'I don't want to train, there's boys in the area, I'm scared' … all kinds of excuses. But it's all about encouraging them to have goals and to go for them."

There's certainly a feeling at thinkBeyond Talent that UK sport contains many more athletes like Richardson-Walsh and Thompson-Smith who want to make social change part of their stories. For whatever reason, those individuals have struggled to find their voice or to be heard thus far. Maybe that's due to a sense of "British reserve," or uncertainty around the impact they could have. For others, it could be a fear of negative reactions or even indifference—there's often a "who cares?" response expressed on social media, particularly on an issue like LGBT representation in sport. "We have to ignore them and carry on with what we're doing," says Richardson-Walsh.

The advice to athletes from Baroness Grey-Thompson, who has been a crossbencher in the House of Lords since 2010, is to be clear what you want to achieve and do it with personality. "I have an opinion on everything, but the world doesn't need to hear all of them," she says with a smile. For those closer to the conclusions of their sporting careers, the ability to focus on a new goal takes on even more importance. "It's that transition—what's next? You need other things to think about." Jones-Hall cites the example of Andy Murray, for whom injury is forcing a finale in tennis at the age of just 31, as a reminder of the sharp shock of impending retirement. As a long-standing vocal champion for gender equality, his views are guaranteed to be sought out after the big serves have stopped, on matters inside and outside the tramlines.

What about our other modern-day idols, particularly those in the Premier League? Their community work often tends to go unsung, while in many cases, players' social accounts are managed almost to the point of sanitisation. The impact made by Raheem Sterling's polemic on undercurrents of racism in the media had added power because it felt so rare for a footballer to make such a strong statement. "I'm sure there would be a lot of footballers who have things close to their heart which, if they were given the choice, they would probably stand up for," says Richardson-Walsh. "It's interesting why more of them don't do it.

"Agents and management companies can play a massive part in that, just by asking the question—have you thought about this? Is there anything that you're really passionate about, a campaign you want to fight for?"

Thompson-Smith may not be a household name just yet, but it won't be long until Olympics fever is again building in the national consciousness. Grasping all the opportunities which that presents is the next level. "The job is more than just sport, it's about inspiring people," she says confidently. As more athletes find their feet in the arena of social causes, the climb towards equality continues to gather pace.

14

Sports Offers a Path to the Presidency

Sam Riches

Sam Riches is a writer and a journalist living in Canada. His work has appeared online at the New Yorker, Wired, *The Athletic, Salon. com, the Classical, and elsewhere.*

In the following viewpoint, Sam Riches compares sports and politics. Each endeavor, he writes, is performative in nature, and provides a source of patriotism, as teams compete against each other, "whether it's the Yankees and Red Sox, or Democrats and Republicans." Their followers are comprised of devoted, loyal supporters, and, like politicians, athletes are constantly subjected to analysis and critique. Athletes also have the ability to influence society. As Riches notes, nearly every president has had some connection to the sports world. Presidential hopefuls use sports as a campaign tool through which they can promote themselves as active and healthy participants, or spectators who share a passion with the average American.

O n the eve of the 2008 presidential election, during ESPN's *Monday Night Football* broadcast, which averages nearly 10 million viewers a week, two separate interviews with candidates Barack Obama and John McCain were beamed into homes across the country.

In each conversation McCain and Obama spoke of their connection to the sports world and rattled off ideas to improve it. "I

"Want to Be the President? Start Playing Sports," by Sam Riches, The Social Justice Foundation. April 16, 2015. Reprinted by permission of Pacific Standard.

was a mediocre junior varsity linebacker and so I have the greatest respect and admiration for those who display these incredible skills on the football field," said McCain, before speaking out for more regulations against performance enhancing drugs.

Obama, meanwhile, lamented the state of his hometown— and injury riddled—Chicago Bears before saying he'd like to see a playoff system implemented in college football, which, at that time, did not yet exist.

The interviews were light-hearted, mostly softball questions lobbed up for easy answers, but both candidates used the platform to frame their connection to sport, and in turn absorb the connotations often associated with it—nobility and nationalism, herculean individual effort and personal sacrifice for team success, an apt metaphor for the prospective leader of any nation.

Eight hours after the interviews aired, the polls opened in the Eastern states. Then, in 2012, Obama returned to *Monday Night Football*, this time flanked by Mitt Romney and once again, on the eve of the election, the conversation turned to sports.

Teddy Roosevelt, an avid hunter and perhaps America's most rugged president, was known to orchestrate impromptu boxing and wrestling matches in the White House. That ended when, at 50 years old, an anonymous sparring partner landed a strike to Roosevelt that detached the retina in his left eye. This sort of macho posturing is one of the many traits shared between athletics and politics.

Each world is performative in nature, wrung out as a source of patriotism, with teams competing against each other, whether it's the Yankees and Red Sox, or Democrats and Republicans. Their bases are formed of devoted, loyal supporters, and athletes, like politicians, are constantly subjected to analysis and critique. They also have an ability to effect change through the culture of stardom that surrounds them.

William Taft, in 1910, was the first president to throw the opening pitch at a baseball game. Now, with the practice dating back more than 100 years, the pitches draw comparisons, a physical act to chart the perceived masculinity of a former president. Just this week a GIF juxtaposing Obama and George Bush's pitches reached the top of Reddit.

Bush, notably, was also the co-owner of the Texas Rangers before he was president, and, in his younger days, the head cheerleader at his high school. His father, meanwhile, was the captain of his high school's baseball and soccer teams and the first baseman for Yale's varsity team. Keeping in baseball, Bush junior was also on the wrong end of an oft-told joke during his political career: "He was born on third base and thinks he hit a triple."

And there's the shared connection to pop culture. Ronald Reagan, an actor who also played college football, had a seminal role in the 1940 film *Knute Rockne, All American,* where he played the role of George Gipp, a halfback at Notre Dame. When his character tells his teammates to "win just one for the Gipper," he unknowingly spoke the rallying cry his supporters would use during his bid for presidency.

The list goes on, with examples to be found for nearly every president. Arguably the most accomplished president, athletically, was Gerald Ford, who was an all-state athlete in high school football and played center and linebacker for the University of Michigan, capturing consecutive national titles in two undefeated seasons in 1932 and '33.

Despite Ford's accomplishments in sports, Obama has become known as the "sports president," which has more to do with the era of his presidency, and his sport of choice, than any glaring feats of athleticism. Whether he's filling out an NCAA bracket on national television or playing pick-up basketball with NBA athletes, the details are shared over social and mainstream media, and absorbed by a fan base, in basketball, that is younger and more engaged online than others.

But as the previous examples have shown and time will surely demonstrate, Obama is not the first president to be interested in sports—and he won't be the last. Future championship teams will continue the tradition of visiting the White House and whoever they shake hands with will once again benefit from a shared moment in pop culture and relevancy that, however briefly, reaches beyond politics and into entertainment.

By appearing at games, or offering commentary on past matches, presidents are taking part in a shared experience with fellow Americans. Their presence at sporting events is a reminder of this common ground, of normality. It's a place where, beyond politics, an emotional connection can be made.

If, for example, Obama makes a joke at the expense of a team you cheer for, it's more endearing than anything else because he's following in line with traditional fandom. In that moment the boundary of "president" fades, and Obama appears as a fan, free of any other connotation.

That relatability, especially in politics, is essential. Politicians will often pull on sports metaphors for this purpose, but, just as anything else, that can backfire. Last year Obama was criticized for saying his policies in Syria and Ukraine were meant to "avoid errors," a reference to baseball.

"You hit singles, you hit doubles; every once in a while we may be able to hit a home run," Obama said. "But we steadily advance the interests of the American people and our partnership with folks around the world."

This drew the ire of those who disagreed with his baseball phraseology.

"A singles hitter doesn't scare anybody," Maureen Dowd wrote in the *New York Times*. "It doesn't feel like leadership. It doesn't feel like you're in command of your world." Perhaps Obama should have referenced a grand slam.

There is some posturing to all of this, of course; it's authenticity drummed up to normalize politicians. They are associating themselves with something fun and current and that gives them extra points for likability. Sports serve as a PR tool, to that end, which is not to diminish the politicians that earnestly take interest in athletics, but to take it for what it often is: a politician campaigning.

Hillary Clinton, who formally announced her presidential candidacy on Sunday, knows this as well as anyone. In 2012, alongside ESPN president John Skipper, Clinton introduced the US Department of State and espnW Global Sports Mentoring Program. "Its purpose to connect international and American women with sustainable sports opportunities."

"Sports helped me to learn how to be part of a team," Clinton said. "It also helped me learn how to lose. You can't win every time you go out, and you have to figure out what you're made of after you do lose and whether you're ready to get up and keep going."

Here, Clinton was able to use a familiar trope of sport to her benefit, of getting knocked down and getting back up again, a common refrain and a universally known feeling, that resonates with both sports fans and non-fans alike.

There is the health side to all of this too. Sports are, after all, a form of exercise, and being involved with them gives off the impression of someone who is healthy, both in body and mind. Physical attractiveness plays a role in both worlds, probably more so than we'd care to admit, but for politicians, in particular, appearance matters.

During the 2008 presidential debate, Obama was self-assured, his hands gesturing emphatically as his voice boomed forward. In opposition, McCain seemed tired, disinterested, even frail. Obama appeared ready to lead and strong enough to do it, while questions about McCain's health and age were included in the resulting coverage. This was not to his benefit.

A 2011 study in *Political Psychology* found voters typically view attractive candidates more favorably, though some voters "correct" for the bias of physical appearance. In most circumstances however, attractive candidates were viewed in a more positive light.

The size of the politician also plays a role in voting. A study published last year in *Equality, Diversity and Inclusion: An International Journal*, found that the heft of the politician can sway voters. Using data from 49 senate elections in 2008 and 77 elections in 2012, the researchers found a voting bias against heavier candidates. While obese candidates were largely absent from the data pool, the results showed that thinner counterparts receive a larger percentage of the vote share, and the larger the size difference between the candidates, the larger the vote share discrepancy.

At the rate that images are now disseminated, the politics of appearance matter. By using sports, not only as a campaign tool but as a celebrated cultural practice, politicians come across as active and healthy and engaged with the average citizen, ulterior motives aside. As the next election approaches, more stories of sports and politics will collide, the presidential race itself taking the shape of an athletic spectacle—the horse race—which, all things considered, is fitting. As Richard Nixon once said, "I don't know anything that builds the will to win better than competitive sports."

15

Female Athletes Deserve Equal Pay

Elizabeth Broderick

Elizabeth Broderick is Human Rights Council Special Rapporteur and Independent Expert on discrimination against women in law and practice. Prior to that, she was the longest serving Sex Discrimination Commissioner (2007–2015) in Australia. She is also the founder and convener of "Male Champions of Change."

Elite female athletes do not earn salaries on par with their male counterparts. To justify the disparity, many have argued that women's sports fail to draw the same attention (ticket sales, advertisers, and sponsors) or to have the level of athletic success that men's sports do. But this notion has been debunked by such superstars as tennis's Serena Williams—arguably one of the greatest athletes of either gender in any sport, period—and the USA women's national soccer team, which is the most successful team in international women's soccer. Reconsidering women's sports at all levels is the first step toward equality.

The gender pay gap in sport in Australia is enormous. According to the Workplace Gender Equality Agency, the total remuneration gap for full-time employees is currently 31.5% in the "Sports and Physical Recreation Activities" workforce.

But this is about to change. Earlier this week, The Male Champions of Change (MCC) Sport released their "Pathway to Pay

"Closing the Pay Gap in Sports: Q&A with Elizabeth Broderick AO," by Elizabeth Broderick, BroadAgenda, February 21, 2019. http://www.broadagenda.com.au/home/pay-equity-in-sports-q-and-a-with-elizabeth-broderick/. Licensed under CC BY-ND 4.0.

Equality"—a significant joint initiative, which details the specific actions needed to close the gender pay gap. Bringing together the CEOs of Australia's leading sports organisations, the MCC Sport Group is committed to reducing the overall gap, and taking immediate action to address any unjustifiable difference in "like-for-like" roles in corporate and administrative roles.

Today in this wide-ranging interview, BroadAgenda Editor Dr. Pia Rowe talks to Elizabeth Broderick AO, founder of the globally applauded "Male Champions of Change" initiative, Special Rapporteur in the UN, and Australia's longest serving Sex Discrimination Commissioner (2007–2015).

Q1. As you mention in your new report, Male Champions of Change Pathway to Pay Equality, when it comes to gender pay inequity in sport, we're talking about centuries of underinvestment in women's sports—what was the catalyst for this work, why now?

I think the catalyst for the work was an increased understanding amongst the Male Champions of Change Sport that, if we were to address gender inequality in sport, we needed to go to the pointy end of the issue, and that was pay equality for elite female athletes. We had already looked at pay equality in administration and management roles in sport, which is really important, but just as important—and probably more difficult to actually progress—is the gender inequality in pay for female elite athletes, particularly when compared to their male counterparts.

Q2. What about the community attitudes more broadly—the report lists several arguments against pay equity and you provide evidence for why they don't stack up. How prevalent are these assumptions in the broader community?

It depends on which sports you're looking at. Some sports have been on this journey for quite a long period of time. I'd definitely put sports like tennis and basketball and rowing, and more recently cricket in that category.

Tennis for example, has done a great job ensuring equal pay, equal exposure and equal investment at the elite level. They also do a lot to help people understand the value and uniqueness of the women's game. You can't argue about the payback on that investment when 20 million people in Japan alone tuned in to watch the Australian Open Women's final this year!

And then you have sports, like football and rugby, where elite leagues for women are only just getting off the ground in the context of a very strong legacy of male-only players.

The question for the CEOs was whether continuing this way—with a focus on men's game only—would make them strong in the future. I think that every one of the Male Champions agreed that the future was about sports for everyone, everywhere and that included men and women equally. The question is how to get to that place.

The group also understood that this is a hugely complex area to solve, so pay equality for female athletes is not going to come about next week or even next year. It will take time. However, in setting a strong pathway, using the best knowledge we have of what it takes, each sport aims to accelerate the pace of that change.

So, what the report does is make the task very tangible. Pay equality moves from a pipe dream to an achievable reality. We set out an approach, we provide a broad baseline assessment for each sport and they have committed to tracking and publicly reporting progress annually.

Q3. Last year in particular, there was a lot of media attention around the topic of prize money, especially when a junior surf event awarded the female winner half the amount of their male counterpart. World Surf League ended up announcing equal prize money for men and women, but this issue is far bigger than that. There is a whole ecosystem that exists before you even get to that point. At what point does this shift occur—that girls

and women, despite doing the same sport, training as hard, simply aren't worth as much?

I was really pleased to see that shift because the logic was irrefutable, and it was great to see the power of the community in achieving that change.

The report argues that each sport has to maintain a focus at each point of the Pathway in order to deliver pay equality.

We're looking at the grassroots, so when a parent enrolls their children in the local sporting club, their daughter has access to the same experience as their son. In many sporting organisations this still doesn't happen.

One of the concerns I have as the former Sex Discrimination Commissioner and now as the Special Rapporteur in the UN, is that we are still both explicitly and implicitly sending messages to young girls right from a very early age that maybe they're not valued equally to boys.

This is not a message we want to send to our nation. So, in sport, we want to work from the grassroots right up to the elite level.

Another valuable element of the Pathway is that we unpick what the work of being an elite athlete looks like, breaking it into "work units." We essentially break it down from a payment's perspective—training payments, match payments, appearance payments, media payments. You are able to show where the work requirement is actually equal and where fair and reasonable pay should be an expectation.

If you're a key player that draws fans to the game, you might get an extra allowance. If you or your team attract bigger audiences, you might get extra pay or a loading on top of the base pay. But the base pay should be equal because the work is equal.

So, it asks those questions—are men and women paid equally for these equal units of work, and if not, is there a very good reason for differential payment. It really makes transparent the whole pay structure of sport.

Q4. The gender pay gap in "Sports and Physical Recreation Activities" workforce is 31.5% for full time employees—do we know how Australia stacks up against the rest of the world?

I don't think we know. Australia is actually one of the only countries in the world that captures this type of data. In developing the report, we looked internationally for any other nations that had actually brought all the heads of their national sporting organisations together to act as a united front on pay equality, and we couldn't find any other nations that have done this.

That was another reason to go ahead with the work and develop a strong conceptual framework to understand this and address this issue. And this framework, which we call "Pathway to Pay Equality" will be very useful, not just here in Australia, but in other nations across the world.

Q5. Let's talk about the role of affirmative action briefly, because we know that as soon as the term comes up, it brings up the concept of merit. In your report you discuss methods such as providing a higher base rate to account for the fact that there may initially be fewer opportunities to compete, or less sponsorship dollars available to elite women athletes. The opponents of affirmative action often argue that it undermines the merit principle. How would you respond to that?

The term "affirmative action" sometimes has negative connotations for some, but the way we use it is just to state what is obvious and that is that for a number of sports, they've had a hundred years of unequal investment in the men's game. If we are to move to a situation of pay equality, then it may be necessary in certain instances to redress that inequality by setting a higher base bay for women in certain areas. For example, where an elite level women's competition may be in an establishment phase in a sport and players may have few opportunities to be paid for their "work units" compared to their male counterparts.

We're not prescriptive about that. All we're saying is that we recognise that there may be a case for affirmative action in certain situations, particularly if we want to accelerate the pace at which a women's sport moves from amateur to semi to fully professional.

It's pretty clear that athletes who have the means to dedicate their entire week to their sport have an advantage over those forced to fit training and playing in around earning a living outside of sport.

Q6. What about the language we use? Often, you still hear people talk about "women's sports," whereas men's sport is just "sport," which runs the risk of reinforcing the male norm. Should we think about getting rid of the gendered distinction?

I'm all in favour of talking about sports for everyone, and not making the distinction, but what I would not want to do, is to lose sight of the inequality that currently exists by grouping sport all together.

Often when we're just talking about sports in general, we go back to what the default position has been, and that is that many elite sports focus on men, it's not on men and women equally.

So, I don't want to lose the focus on ensuring that women can access, participate in, develop, have coaching opportunities, and have the opportunities to compete as an elite athlete and be celebrated in the same way as men do. We can't lose that.

Q7. Finally, how close (or far!) are we to achieving pay equity in sports? Is it possible to estimate how many years it will take before we reach the goal?

I don't think I can put an exact year on it because all sports have different starting positions. What I am sure we can do, is make significant progress so that in five years we'll look back and say: "well that was when we drew a line in the sand," and said we were no longer happy [to] tolerate gender inequality in sport and large differences between men and women in equal pay as elite athletes.

And if there are differences, then they need to be differences which everyone in the community would say "yep, that should be different," so they should be justifiable differences.

One great thing about the report is that it describes how there's only certain things that the clubs themselves or the national sporting organisations can control. They can control certain levers and they need to move ahead with those levers, but that's why this report was important because it reached out to other stakeholders like government, the broadcasters, the corporate sponsors, the players' associations, the fans—and reminded everyone that every one of us plays a part in delivering pay equality for elite athletes. By themselves the sporting organisations are not able to do that, to deliver pay equality. What we need is everyone working in the same direction.

It's a call to action, a call to those other stakeholders to step up with the sporting organisations to make pay equality a reality. So far, the reaction has been incredibly positive.

16

Athletes Have an Obligation to Be Leaders

Teresa Wippel

Teresa Wippel is a communications professional based in the Greater Seattle, Washington, area. She is the publisher of Lynwood Today, MLTNews, and My Edmonds News.

Former NBA player Spencer Haywood advocates for using celebrity as an opportunity to effect change. "I think you have to agitate," he said. "If people don't know, they just don't know." He should know: Haywood fought for the right of high school basketball players to go straight to the NBA. His case went to the US Supreme Court, which ruled in his favor in 1971. Haywood also believes that balance is important, that athletes should not lose sight of their goals in the drive to be activists.

When he began his fight in 1970 to play in the National Basketball League before finishing college, former basketball star Spencer Haywood's mission was to provide financial support to his mother and nine siblings who were living "dirt poor" and picking cotton in Mississippi.

In the end, though, his successful legal battle—which started when he joined the Seattle SuperSonics and went all the way to the US Supreme Court—paved the way for opportunities for future NBA players.

"'You Have to Speak Out': Spencer Haywood Addresses Athletics and Activism at MLK Jr. Day Event," by Teresa Wippel, My Edmonds News, January 12, 2018. https://myedmondsnews.com/2018/01/speak-spencer-haywood-addresses-athletics-activism-martin-luther-king-jr-day-event/. Licensed under CC BY 3.0.

"I stood up for the rights of players but deep down it wasn't for the rights of players," Haywood told a standing-room-only crowd gathered Thursday at Edmonds Community College for the school's Martin Luther King Jr. Day program titled "Athletes and Activism." "It was for the rights of my mother to get out of that cotton field, for my family to get off those knees."

The 68-year-old Haywood received a standing ovation when he first walked onto the Black Box Theater stage and again at the end of his appearance. He spent the first part of the program answering questions from the program host—appropriately Edmonds CC men's basketball player Devin Price—and then fielded questions from the audience.

Haywood talked about growing up as one of 10 children, picking cotton in Silver City, Mississippi. "The deal was, if you could work for a full day you could get paid $2 a day from sunup to sundown," he said. "That's where I learned work ethic because you were working for your food, working for your family."

"We didn't have much. We just were very dirt poor," [Haywood] continued, describing how the family's Christmas gifts came in February, not in December. "We had to wait until all the kids threw away their toys and we'd pull the toys out of the junkyard and put them all back together and my mother would declare Christmas on that day," he said.

He described playing in his first high school game after moving to Detroit, Mich., and putting the ball in the wrong basket. He eventually led his high school team to the state championship.

From 1967–68, the 6-foot-9 Haywood played at Trinidad State Junior College in Trinidad, Colo., where he averaged 28.2 points and 22.1 rebounds per game. He was tried out and was chosen to play for the 1968 USA Summer Olympics basketball team in Mexico City after Kareem Abdul-Jabbar decided to boycott the games. "They needed a center," he recalled. "I was in the right place at the right time."

Haywood ended up being the leading scorer for the Olympic team, which won a gold medal.

As a college freshman playing in the Olympics, Haywood said he was "hanging on the outer edge" of the racial unrest that was rocking the nation. In addition to peaceful protests led by Dr. King and others, boxer Muhammad Ali in 1967 was convicted of draft evasion after refusing to be drafted into the Vietnam War on religious grounds. (That conviction was overturned by the US Supreme Court.) African American track and field Olympic medalists Tommie Smith and John Carlos raised black-gloved fists during the summer games in a Black Power salute, to draw attention to inequality in the US.

At the time, Haywood said he remembered thinking: "One of these days, when it becomes my turn, I will stand up. But this is not the right time because we are trying to win a gold medal for this country. And there's nothing like winning a gold medal for America," he said.

After the Olympics, Haywood played his sophomore year at the University of Detroit, where he scored 32.1 points and 21.5 rebounds per game. Because the NBA had a rule that a player could not play there until he was four years out of high school, Haywood went to the ABA's Denver Rockets, where he led the league with 30 points and 19 boards per game, was named Rookie of Year and also the league's Most Valuable Player.

In 1970, Haywood joined the Seattle SuperSonics. "When I arrived in Seattle that day, I said to (Sonics owner) Sam Schulman, this place is like a postcard, so beautiful," Haywood said. He said he also felt warmly welcomed by the city's residents, and it encouraged him to take legal action against the NBA.

"The people in Seattle were different than any place I'd ever been," Haywood said." It felt right then, this is the right place to take on this case. It's going to be a tough case and I need that support."

He eventually won a favorable US Supreme Court decision 7–2 in March 1971, opening the door to high school players entering the NBA. But he faced a storm of controversy a few games into his first season, when the NBA served him with an injunction stating that he couldn't play. "They let me get out on floor, let me get ready for a jump ball and then announced that the game was being played under protest because there was an illegal player on the floor."

The reaction was brutal. Away teams wouldn't play when Haywood was on the floor, fans booed and threw things. One time in Cincinnati, he was escorted out of the arena and had to stand outside in the snow until it was time for the team bus to arrive.

"I knew I was doing the right thing because at that time my mom and my brothers and sisters were still picking cotton in Mississippi," Haywood said. "My mom had been picking cotton and chopping cotton since she was 3 years old and her back went out. She was crawling on the ground picking cotton.

"So that was the whole motivation for the fight that was to come."

Program moderator Devin Price asked Haywood for his take on the status of NFL quarter Colin Kaepernick, who began protesting racial injustice by not standing while the National Anthem was being played before the start of games. In 2017, Kaepernick filed a grievance against the NFL and its owners, accusing them of colluding to not hire him.

"Of course he (Kaepernick) is being blackballed for leading the protests, but he was doing it for the right reasons," Haywood said.

During the 1974–75 season, Haywood helped lead the Sonics to their first playoff berth. Overall, during his five seasons with Seattle, Haywood averaged 24.9 points per game and 12.1 rebounds per game. In 1975, the Sonics traded him to the New York Knicks, and he also later played for the New Orleans Jazz, Los Angeles Lakers, and Washington Bullets.

During the late 1970s, Haywood had drug problems that caused him to be suspended from the Lakers, and he played in Italy for a year before returning to the NBA to play two seasons with the Bullets. (He addressed this issue briefly during the audience Q&A, stating that he had been sober for 31 years.)

The Sonics retired Haywood's No. 24 jersey on Feb. 26, 2007, and Haywood has remained loyal to his Seattle roots. When he was inducted into the Basketball Hall of Fame in 2015, Haywood said the NBA encouraged him to be represented as a player from the New York Knicks, Denver Nuggets or even the Oklahoma Thunder (where the Sonics team moved to in 2008). The reasoning was, those franchises are active and he would get revenue from jersey sales. But Haywood was firm that he wanted to go into the Hall of Fame as a Seattle Supersonic.

"I owe it to Seattle to be a Sonic," he said.

Haywood said he's hopeful, given all the recent talk of bringing both a professional hockey and basketball team to Seattle soon, that "we'll get a chance to bring the NBA back."

"Sonics are forever and trust me, we're coming back," Haywood said to audience applause. "Soon, very soon."

Answering another question from Price, Haywood said that athletes have an obligation to be leaders and role models. He pointed to current player LeBron James, who started a foundation that has funded putting 1,000 students through college. Haywood said that James and several other current players also pledged to donate $17 million annually to fund health insurance for the NBA's Retired Players Association (which also covers WNBA and Harlem Globetrotters players). Haywood currently serves as chair.

An audience member asked whether athletes should do more to highlight discrimination against Muslims and Latinos. Haywood agreed, noting that his first wife, the model Iman, was from Somalia and he was a practicing Muslim during their 12-year marriage.

Another questioner asked his opinion about the importance of activism. "I think you have to agitate," he said "You have to speak out, you have to make things right because if people don't know, they just don't know. How do you get out there to step out and help them know?"

How would Haywood encourage young men today to engage in activism, one attendee asked. "You do your best for yourself and I think you have to be a little careful that you don't get so swallowed up in your activism that you lose what your goals are," Haywood replied. "The balance is what it's all about. And love each other, because you are each other and that's all you have."

17

Caster Semenya Has Raised Questions About Sex, Gender, Race, and Fairness in Sports

Shuaib Manjra

Shuaib Manjra is a sports physician. He serves on the board of the South African Institute for Drug-Free Sport and was a chairperson of the Medical Commission of the South African Sports Confederation and Olympic Committee (SASCOC). He writes in his personal capacity.

Is it fair for an athlete with unusual variances of certain hormones that might enhance performance to compete against those who do not? How can a sporting organization or council regulate such categories as sex and gender without raising deeper ethical issues? South African runner Caster Semenya has proven herself a champion among women runners, but her success raised eyebrows and prompted sex verification testing by the International Association of Athletics Federations (IAAF). These actions have been derided as sexist and racist by many.

Caster Semenya's case has generated global interest. It has raised questions about sex, gender, race and fairness in sport.

This is not the first high-profile South African athlete that the Council for Arbitration in Sport (CAS) has had to consider. It also had to decide whether Oscar Pistorius could participate in "able-bodied events." The argument, then, against Pistorius's participation was that his running blades gave him an unfair advantage. But the CAS decided that it did not. Now it has to decide whether Semenya's biology gives her an unfair advantage in women's athletics.

The CAS will deliberate on the proposed IAAF policy titled Eligibility Regulations for the Female Classification (Athletes with Differences of Sex Development). It will address athletes who do not fit into the binary sexual categories used in sports.

The IAAF has a tough job ensuring a level playing field for all athletes. No doubt enormous effort to balance various interests and rights has gone into producing its policy.

Currently sport recognizes four bases for differentiation: sex (male/female), weight (in sports such as boxing, weightlifting and judo), age (in age-specific competitions), and degree of impairment (in disabled sport). Possibly the only sport that doesn't differentiate on sex is equestrian.

With established categories an athlete who crosses into another category is penalised by recategorisation. This is understandable for weight and in most cases for age, which is often a challenge in countries with poor birth registration systems. Degree of impairment in disabled sport is a fine balance between an objective and subjective assessment and often the assumed advantage is speculative. A higher category in disabled sport results in significant disadvantage to the athlete.

In the case of sex (not to be confused with gender), the binary division is not helpful for some athletes who cross the established boundaries. This is one of the critical issues that the CAS will consider in its ruling on the IAAF policy: How do we differentiate sex and what is the best marker?

Various methods have been attempted previously—including a nude parade by female athletes to assess external genitalia, analysis of chromosomal patterns, hormonal profiles, assessment of internal genitalia, and a combination of these—but the issue remains fraught because these analyses only throw up greater questions.

Challenges, acknowledged by the IAAF, include mixed chromosomal types, androgen insensitivity syndrome and alpha-reductase deficiency (genetically males but with female characteristics). These cases make binary classification notoriously difficult and sport has no special category for these athletes. Importantly, many of these athletes are unaware of this difference, and are frequently picked up on when they test for elevated testosterone levels.

The IAAF policy attempts to answer this complex question by reducing it to a single end-point variable: female testosterone (fT) levels. The CAS will have to address this challenging question.

Accepting the fact that some females have elevated testosterone (fT) levels for a whole range of reasons, the second question that the CAS will consider is: Do athletes with elevated fT have an advantage?

This is the question that the CAS posed to the IAAF in the Dutee Chand case in 2015 when suspending the IAAF's previous regulation—Regulations Governing Eligibility of Females with Hyperandrogenism to Compete in Women's Competition—granting it two years to provide evidence. The court accepted that some female athletes have higher testosterone levels but questioned whether this translates into physiological and performance advantage and therefore could be used as a basis for remedial action by the IAAF.

The IAAF policy is based on population norms (with an allowance for athletes) where male and female levels of testosterone do not overlap. The statistically normal range of testosterone in females is 0.1–2 nmol/l and in males it is between 7.7 and 30 nmol/l. Testosterone is considered the major differentiator in sports performance between males and females: male performances exceed female performances between 9-15%.

It is fair to assume that athletes such as Chand and Semenya have levels greater than 10 nmol/l since both were compelled by the IAAF to reduce their levels under the previous policy where the testosterone ceiling for athletes classified as female was pegged at 10 nmol/l (the new policy proposes a more stringent cut-off of 5 nmol/l). It is also fair to assume that the IAAF believes that raised testosterone levels grant female athletes with elevated fT a physiological and performance advantage. A paper published in the *British Journal of Sports Medicine* by the IAAF that compared athletes with high T to low T, demonstrated an advantage only in the 400m, 400m hurdles, 800m, hammer throw, and pole vault.

This raises the next critical question that the CAS will consider: if there is indeed an advantage, what is its quantum (size)? Of all the events considered, the referenced paper showed an advantage of 2.73% (400 m), 2.78% (400 m hurdles), 1.78% (800 m), 4.53% (hammer throw), and 2.94% (pole vault). It has been estimated that if Semenya was to reduce her T levels, it would affect her performance negatively in the region of 5%. This is assumed to have occurred when, in compliance with the previous IAAF policy, Semenya did attempt to reduce her fT levels through hormonal manipulation.

This would trigger the next question: what is a tolerable level of advantage? What level of fT would not grant a female athlete an unfair advantage? There must be a cut-off defined scientifically by the IAAF. (As mentioned, previously it was 10 nmol/l and now it is 5 nmol/l). But these cut-off values relate to fT levels and not a performance threshold, since the demonstrable advantage of elevated fT does not exceed 5% according to the IAAF's own study.

The final question is what is considered an unfair advantage? Many accidents of nature are automatically classified as fair advantages: height, muscle composition, arm span, feet size, etc.

But such category comparisons are spurious since sports does not classify according to these criteria but does differentiate by sex. On the one hand athletes with different sexual development have no control over the advantage they gain, unlike doping. On the other hand evidence from the East German dataset of state sponsored doping in the 1970s demonstrated a significant benefit to female athletes doping with testosterone. The CAS may ask: if there is indeed an advantage, where would the line signifying an unfair advantage lie: Would a 10 or 20% advantage be considered unfair?

The CAS will have to grapple with these five questions, and the evidence supporting the various positions in its deliberations. The results will be made public before the end of March 2019.

The weaknesses in the IAAF case have already been exposed: the paper which forms the fundamental basis of their case has fatal flaws and has been panned by academics and statisticians. The authors themselves have acknowledged the flaws, and they had to produce an addendum to the paper.

The first flaw is that there were errors compiling their dataset (with an error rate potentially as high as 30%). The second flaw is that the study compared high fT with low fT athletes, not with normal fT athletes.

There's also a flaw in the IAAF policy: while the article demonstrated advantage in specific events, the IAAF added additional events to their policy without scientific evidence, including all races between 400m and the one-mile. This was despite there being no evidence of advantage demonstrated in races above 800m. Also, the field events, where there is demonstrable advantage in the IAAF study, are excluded.

But it could also be argued that since testosterone increases muscle strength, power, endurance and speed, enhances cardiorespiratory function, and causes elevated red blood cell volume, it would grant advantage in all events and not only those selected by the IAAF.

Finally, despite its denial the IAAF policy attempts to assign sex, evidenced by the title of its policy: "Eligibility regulations for the female classification."

The perennial racism question has been bandied around. Notwithstanding a remark by Olympic official Norman Cox, over fifty years ago, that there should be a separate category for black female athletes who are "unfairly advantaged hermaphrodites," the

IAAF has equally applied its standard to white and black athletes. A white athlete will testify as an expert witness for Caster on the negative effects of reducing her testosterone levels. European athletes have fallen foul of the regulations, notwithstanding the fact that the two latest high profile cases happen to be black.

The South African Department of Sport and Recreation has wagered a whopping R25-million on this case. The key challenge lies in CAS balancing genetics, anatomy, physiology, endocrinology and performance, against fairness and gender rights in their decision. Even 29 experts will not enable the CAS to produce a result that is satisfactory to all, and this case may just find itself in a higher civil court if it finds in favour of the IAAF. The emotional cost to Caster Semenya, Dutee Chand and similar athletes has been extremely high.

Organizations to Contact

The editors have compiled the following list of organizations concerned with the issues debated in this book. The descriptions are derived from materials provided by the organizations. All have publications or information available for interested readers. The list was compiled on the date of publication of the present volume; the information provided here may change. Be aware that many organizations take several weeks or longer to respond to inquiries, so allow as much time as possible.

Athlete Ally
325 W. 38th St., Room 305
New York NY 10018
(212) 213-1462
website: www.athleteally.org/

Athlete Ally endorses the idea that everyone should have equal access, opportunity, and experience in sports—regardless of one's sexual orientation, gender identity or gender expression. Its goal is to end the rampant homophobia and transphobia in sport and to activate the athletic community to exercise their leadership to champion LGBTQ equality. The website contains numerous resources about LGBTQ inclusion in the sports world.

Athletes for a Better World (ABW)
2997 Cobb Parkway SE, Ste. 300, #723175
Atlanta, GA 31139
(678) 523-5839
email: bcatherman@abw.org
website:www.abw.org

Athletes for a Better World advocates a "Code of Living" in order to promote discipline, integrity, respect, cooperation, and compassion among athletes. The group publishes free educational materials as well as a quarterly newsletter.

Center for the Study of Sport in Society
101 Belvidere St.
Boston, MA 02115
(617) 373-4025
website: www.northeastern.edu/sportinsociety/

The Center for the Study of Sport in Society educates and supports emerging leaders and organizations in sports. It provides the awareness, knowledge, and skills needed to implement innovative and impactful solutions for social change. Areas of focus include: leadership, healthy development, diversity and inclusion, violence prevention, community building, community service, and civic engagement.

Colin Kaepernick Foundation
website: www.kaepernick7.com

Colin Kaepernick created the Colin Kaepernick Foundation, a nonprofit organization that focuses on fighting oppression through education and social activism. The Million Dollar Pledge, a program in which Kaepernick vowed to donate $1 million to charity, has been a key component of the organization. Kaepernick has donated to a large number of causes, including Mothers Against Police Brutality, School on Wheels and Youth Services, Inc. Kaepernick also has established the "Know Your Rights Camp," which raises awareness about higher education, self-empowerment, and instruction about how to properly interact with law enforcement. His website contains articles on the causes Kaepernick supports and the rights for which he is fighting.

The Institute for Diversity and Ethics in Sports (TIDES)
University of Central Florida (UCF)
400 Central Florida Blvd.
Orlando, Florida 32816
(407) 823-4887
email: info@tidesport.org
website: www.tidesport.org/

Run by the UCF College of Business Administration's DeVos Sport Business Mangement Graduate Program, the Institute for Diversity and Ethics in Sports (TIDES) focuses on business skills in the sports industry. The organization specializes in issues related to gender and race in amateur, collegiate, and professional sports.

The LeBron James Family Foundation
3800 Embassy Parkway, Ste. 360
Akron, OH 44333-8389
email: info@lrmrventures.com
website: www.lebronjamesfamilyfoundation.org

The mission of the LeBron James Family Foundation, initiated by basketball superstar LeBron James, is to positively affect the lives of children and young adults through education and co-curricular educational initiatives. The foundation believes that an education and living an active, healthy lifestyle is pivotal to the development of children and young adults.

National Alliance of African American Athletes
P.O. Box 60743
Harrisburg, PA 17106-0743
(717) 312-8162
email: info@naaaa.com
website: www.naaaa.com/

Established in 1989, the vision of the National Alliance of African American Athletes is to be the preeminent organization helping youth achieve academic excellence and reach their highest potential. The mission of the organization is to uplift and mentor youth, focusing on African American males, through programs that prepare students for college. The organization also believes in; leveraging athletes as catalysts to inspire leadership, while recognizing and rewarding academic, athletic, and community excellence.

The National Association of Black Professional Athletes (NABPA)
10130 Perimeter Parkway, Ste. 200
Charlotte, NC 28216
(704) 912-5578
website: www.thenabpa.org/

NABPA is a nonprofit created to provide all active and retired African American Athletes of the NFL, NBA, WNBA, MLB, NHL, MLS, PGA, Professional Tennis, Boxing, and NASCAR with a platform to improve our communities and use their voices to initiative change throughout the world. NABPA will share its global initiative with other black athletes around the world standing as "One Team One Voice" for educational, social justice reform and professional change. NABPA believes that individually their voices resonate, but united they can create a movement of unstoppable proportions.

Women's Sports Foundation (WSF)
247 West 30th St., 5th Floor
New York, NY 10001
(800) 227-3988
email: info@WomensSportsFoundation.org
website: www.womenssportsfoundation.org

The Women's Sports Foundation is dedicated to advancing the lives of girls and women through sports and physical activity. It supports the enforcement of Title IX of the Educational Amendments of 1972, and helps to educate the public through dissemination of facts, statistics, and background data on women in sports.

You Can Play
PO Box 7460
Denver, CO 80207
email: seth@youcanplayproject.org
website: www.youcanplayproject.org

You Can Play is dedicated to ensuring equality, respect and safety for all athletes, without regard to sexual orientation and/or gender identity. The organization works to guarantee that athletes are given a fair opportunity to compete, judged by other athletes and fans alike, and only by what they contribute to the sport or their team's success. You Can Play seeks to challenge the culture of locker rooms and spectator areas by focusing only on an athlete's skills, work ethic and competitive spirit.

Bibliography

Books

Stephen Amidon, *Something Like the Gods: A Cultural History of the Athlete from Achilles to Lebron*. New York: Rodale, 2012.

Raymond Arsenault, *Arthur Ashe: A Life*. New York, NY: Simon & Schuster, 2018.

Arthur Ashe, *Days of Grace*. New York, NY: Random House Publishing Group, 2011.

Amy Bass, *Not the Triumph but the Struggle: The 1968 Olympics and the Making of the Black Athlete*. Minneapolis, MN: University of Minnesota Press, 2004.

James Blake and Carol Taylor, *Ways of Grace: Stories of Activism, Adversity, and How Sports Can Bring Us Together*. New York, NY: Amistad, 2018.

Paddy Dolan and John Connolly, *Sport and National Identities: Globalization and Conflict*. New York, NY: Routledge, 2018.

Marty Gitlin, ed., *Athletes, Ethics, and Morality*. New York, NY: Greenhaven, 2019.

Margaret Haerens and Lynn M. Zott, *Professional Athletes*. Detroit, MI: Greenhaven Press, 2014.

Duchess Harris and Cynthia K. Henzel, *Politics and Protest in Sports*. Minneapolis, MN: Abdo Publishing, 2019.

Simon Henderson, *Sidelined: How American Sports Challenged the Black Freedom Struggle*. Lexington: University Press of Kentucky, 2013.

William T. Hoston, *New Perspectives on Race & Ethnicity: Critical Readings About the Black Experience in Trump's America*. Dubuque, IA: Kendall Hunt Publishing Co., 2018.

Michael Huyghue, *Behind the Line of Scrimmage: Inside the Front Office of the NFL.* New York, NY: Center Street, 2018.

Cathal Kilcline, *Sport and Protest: Global Perspectives.* London: Routledge, 2018.

Gabriel Kuhn, *Playing as If the World Mattered: An Illustrated History of Activism in Sports.* Oakland, CA: PM Press, 2015.

Patrick B. Miller and David K. Wiggins, *Sport and the Color Line: Black Athletes and Race Relations in 20th Century America.* New York, NY: Routledge, 2004.

Louis Moore, *We Will Win the Day: The Civil Rights Movement, the Black Athlete, and the Quest for Equality.* Santa Barbara, CA: Praeger, 2017.

Thomas Riggs, *Are Athletes Good Role Models?* Farmington Hills, MI: Greenhaven Press, 2014.

Kate Shoup, *Billie Jean King: The Battle of the Sexes and Title IX.* New York, NY: Cavendish Square Publishing, 2016.

Danielle Smith-Llera, *Black Power Salute: How a Photograph Captured a Political Protest.* North Mankato, MN: Compass Point Books, 2017.

Lindsey R. Swindall, *Paul Robeson: A Life of Activism and Art.* Landham, MD: Rowman & Littlefield, 2015.

Etan Thomas, *We Matter: Athletes and Activism.* Brooklyn, NY: Akashic Books, 2018.

Mike Yorkey, *Playing with Purpose: Inside the Lives and Faith of the NFL's Most Intriguing Personalities Including Jared Allen, Colin Kaepernick, and Drew Brees.* Uhrichsville, OH: Barbour Publishing, 2013.

Dave Zirin, *A People's History of Sports in the United States: 250 Years of Politics, Protest, People, and Play.* New York, NY: New Press, 2009.

Periodicals and Internet Sources

Raymond Arsenault, "How Arthur Ashe Transformed Tennis—and Athlete Activism, *History*, September 10, 2018. https://www.history.com/news/arthur-ashe-black-tennis-champion-us-open-activism-courage.

"Athletes on the Right?" *Yale News*, February 29, 2008. https://yaledailynews.com/blog/2008/02/29/athletes-on-the-right/.

Jerry Brewer, "Opinion: Sorry for the Inconvenience Fans, but Black Athlete Activism Is Multiplying," *Chicago Tribune,* August 17, 2017. https://www.chicagotribune.com/sports/breaking/ct-black-athlete-activism-is-multiplying-20170817-story.html.

Adam Clymer, "Jack Kemp, Statesman and Athlete," *Seattle Times*, May 3, 2009. https://www.seattletimes.com/seattle-news/politics/jack-kemp-statesman-and-athlete/.

Chas Early, "August 3, 1936: Jesse Owens Wins 100m Gold in Front of Adolf Hitler at the Berlin Olympics," BT, August 3, 2018. https://home.bt.com/news/on-this-day/august-3-1936-jesse-owens-wins-100m-gold-in-front-of-adolf-hitler-at-the-berlin-olympics-11363995389348.

Samuel G. Freedman, "When White Sports Fans Turn on Black Athletes," *The Guardian*, October 25, 2017. https://www.theguardian.com/commentisfree/2017/oct/05/white-sports-fans-nfl-black-athletes-race-protest.

Scott Frostman, "Kneeling During the Anthem Disrespectful to the Nation," *WiscNews*, August 30, 2018. https://www.wiscnews.com/baraboonewsrepublic/opinion/columnists/frostman-column-kneeling-during-the-anthem-disrespectful-to-the-nation/article_7c1d81ef-95c4-5cfa-b260-fb230b60f209.html.

"Future of Sports Activism: Reimagining Its Bottom Line," The Aspen Institute, December 10, 2018. https://www.aspeninstitute.org/events/future-of-sports-activism/.

Sean Gregory, "Maryland's Firing of Football Coach DJ Durkin Marks a Watershed Moment for Athlete Activism," *Time*, November 1, 2018. http://time.com/5441237/maryland-football-coach-firing-athlete-activism/.

Jon Holmes, "Athlete Activism Upsurge Encouraging Next Generation to Speak up for Social Causes," Sky Sports, January 19, 2019. https://www.skysports.com/more-sports/other-sports/news/29877/11610772/athlete-activism-upsurge-encouraging-next-generation-to-speak-up-for-social-causes.

"Inside Look: Tennis Icon & Activist Billie Jean King," Tory Burch Foundation. http://www.toryburchfoundation.org/resources/innovation/get-to-know-billie-jean-king/.

Aman Kidwai, "Etan Thomas Addressed Social Issues Before It Was the Popular Thing to Do," *Washington City Paper*, December 26, 2018. https://www.washingtoncitypaper.com/sports/article/21038546/etan-thomas-addressed-social-issues-before-it-was-the-popular-thing-to-do.

Stephen Moore, "Why Sports and Politics Do Not Mix," *Washington Times,* October 8, 2017. https://www.washingtontimes.com/news/2017/oct/8/sports-and-politics-do-not-mix/.

Armando Salguero, "Dear Sports: Stick to Sports," *Miami Herald*, September 30, 2017. https://www.miamiherald.com/sports/spt-columns-blogs/armando-salguero/article176389926.html.

Sandeep Stanley, "Stanley: LeBron James Should Not 'Shut Up and Dribble,'" *Iowa State Daily,* February 20, 2018. http://www.iowastatedaily.com/opinion/stanley-lebron-james-should-not-shut-up-and-dribble/article_fbaa2f06-1606-11e8-a856-6b142dcc5829.html.

Jess Staufenberg, "Muhammad Ali: Symbol of the Civil Rights Movement," June 4, 2016. https://www.independent.co.uk/

news/uk/home-news/muhammad-ali-symbol-of-the-civil-rights-movement-a7065361.html.

David Andrew Stoler, "The Complicated Activism of Arthur Ashe," Politico, August 29, 2018. https://www.politico.com/magazine/story/2018/08/29/the-careful-complicated-activism-of-arthur-ashe-219610.

Dominique Walker, "OPINION: LeBron James Is Too Important to 'Shut Up and Dribble,'" *The State Hornet*, February 21, 2018. https://statehornet.com/2018/02/opinion-lebron-james-is-too-important-to-shut-up-and-dribble/.

Errin Haines Whack, "Black Athletes Have a Long History of Not Sticking to Sports," The Associated Press, February 2, 2018. https://www.wcpo.com/sports/black-athletes-have-long-history-of-not-sticking-to-sports.

Dave Ziren, "Shut Up and Play? Patriotism, Jock Culture and the Limits of Free Speech," *The Nation*, May 4, 2011. https://www.thenation.com/article/shut-and-play-patriotism-jock-culture-and-limits-free-speech/.

Index

A

Abdul-Jabbar, Kareem, 22, 45, 47, 71, 72, 73, 101

Ali, Muhammad, 7, 8, 12–14, 16, 19, 22, 32, 40–43, 45, 71, 72, 73, 102

Ashe, Arthur, 33, 45, 51

B

Barkley, Charles, 12–14

Battle of the Sexes (tennis), 62

black athletes, 15, 16, 20–24, 27, 33, 42, 44, 75, 76, 110

blacklisting and blackballing, 8, 22, 24, 51, 103

Black Lives Matter, 9, 49, 51

Black Power salute, 15, 37, 48, 102

Boston Celtics (NBA), 76

boxing, 7, 8, 40–43, 44, 88, 107

Boyer, Nate, 7

Boykoff, Jules, 30

brain injuries, 40, 42, 43

brands and branding, 44, 46, 57, 58–61, 78, 82

Broderick, Elizabeth, 93, 94–99

Brown, Jim, 16, 71–74

Brundage, Avery, 31, 32, 33–37

Bryant, Howard, 20–24

Bryant, Kobe, 72

Buffalo Bills (NFL), 10, 53, 55

Bush, George H. W., 44, 46, 47, 50, 53, 54, 55

Bush, George W., 89

C

Carlos, John, 7, 8, 15, 30–38, 48, 102

Carlson, Michael, 53

Carter, Jimmy, 26, 67

Caslavska, Vera, 38–39

Castile, Philando, 9, 18

Chand, Dutee, 108, 111

Chicago Bulls, 21, 45, 46–47, 50

Cleveland Browns (NFL), 9, 72

Clinton, Bill, 53, 56

Clinton, Hillary, 91

Council for Arbitration in Sport (CAS), 106–111

Cox, Norman, 110

Crawford, John, III, 9

Curry, Steph, 8, 17, 76, 77

D

Denver Broncos (NFL), 57, 58

Dole, Bob, 53, 54, 55, 56

E

Edwards, Harry, 23, 32–33

Eisenhower, Dwight D., 29

ESPN, 60, 87, 91